£8 [71479] Michael Leal

Lives in Cricket:

C000263046

Johnny Briggs
Poor Johnny

Stuart Brodkin

First published in Great Britain by
Association of Cricket Statisticians and Historians
Cardiff CF11 9XR

© ACS, 2007

Stuart Brodkin has asserted his right under the Copyright, Designs
and Patents Act 1988 to be identified as the author of the work.

All Rights Reserved. No part of this publication may be
reproduced, stored in a retrieval system, or transmitted in any
form, or by any means, electronic, mechanical, photocopying,
recording or otherwise without the prior permission in writing of
the Copyright holders, nor be otherwise circulated in any form, or
binding or cover other than in which it is published and without a
similar condition including this condition being imposed on the
subsequent publisher.

British Library Cataloguing-in-Publication Data.

A catalogue record for this book is available from the British
Library.

ISBN: 978 1 905138 48 7

Typeset by Limlow Books

Contents

Chapter One
The Last Rites

'Sympathise with all good Lancashire sportsmen in the death of poor little Johnny.' Derbyshire CCC

If it is true that you can measure a man's worth during his lifetime by the numbers who turn out to mark his death, then Johnny Briggs must have been a very remarkable human being indeed.

When Briggs was laid to rest at Stretford Cemetery, a short journey from Old Trafford cricket ground, on Wednesday, 15 January 1902, there were more than 4,000 people present to observe the last rites with at least a thousand of them having travelled by special train from Oxford Road station in Manchester city centre and many hundreds more having made their way there by bicycle and on foot.

It was a dry and overcast day, but there must have been a chill in the air as Briggs' coffin was lowered into the ground. The list of mourners attending the funeral read like a cricketers' Who's Who of the time. Among those present was Lancashire president, former opening batsman and club captain, A.N. 'Monkey' Hornby, who had earlier issued a general invitation – via the *Manchester Guardian* – to Lancashire members to attend the funeral. Also there on that sad day were other well-known names from the cricketing lexicon, including William Gunn (Nottinghamshire), George Hirst (Yorkshire), Walter Sugg (Derbyshire), the Lancashire team, including Walter Sugg's brother Frank, and members of the committee as well as representatives of a number of local teams. Derbyshire sent the following telegram which summed up the feelings of those present: 'Sympathise with all good Lancashire sportsmen in the death of poor little Johnny.' George Robey, the music hall comedian, later knighted, was also present.

Wreaths crowded the graveside, adding a welcome touch of colour to an otherwise sombre scene, and among them was one from Andrew Stoddart, who had captained Briggs in the England team. Stoddart's floral tribute included a knot of ribbon in the colours of

A well-known portrait of Briggs taken in 1888 by Messrs Hawkins of Brighton

the last Test team which had gone out to Australia. George Yates, who played ten seasons with Derbyshire, and his wife sent an emblem in hyacinths of three cricket stumps held together at the top by bails of violet; across the wicket was a bat and ball also made up of violets. Locally-based Broughton Rangers rugby football club sent a wreath in the form of a harp with the club colours attached and Robey's was made up of bay leaves tied with long red and white streamers. There were two wreaths from Widnes, where, as a small boy, Briggs received his early coaching in the game. One of them came from the mayor and town council of the municipal borough. Floral tributes were also sent by Lancashire Police, Derbyshire Cricket Club and the Manchester Press Club, the latter no doubt in grateful thanks to Briggs for the sheer amount of copy he had provided during his career.

The service was conducted by the Rev John Russell Napier, who had played alongside Briggs for Lancashire. At the graveside were

Rev John Russell Napier, who officiated at Briggs' funeral, played alongside Briggs as a fast bowler for Lancashire in two games in 1888, once against Australia at Old Trafford, when he took seven wickets and compiled the top score of 37 in Lancashire's second innings as they won by 23 runs, and against Yorkshire at Sheffield where he took four wickets in 14 deliveries without conceding a run. Preston-born Napier learned his cricket at Marlborough College, going on to play two matches for Cambridge University before, in 1892, helping to steer his local club Walsden, based on the Lancashire-Yorkshire border, into the Central Lancashire League.

Briggs' mournful widow, Alice, and their twin sons, John Hector and George, then aged eight, who had walked in the funeral procession, headed by the glass hearse heaped with flowers containing Briggs' body, from their home in nearby Stamford Street.

Three days earlier, Briggs had passed away quietly in his sleep – at 12 noon on 11 January, 1902 in Cheadle Royal Lunatic Asylum, according to his death certificate. The cause of death was given as 'cerebral disease about two-and-a-half years – general paralysis of the insane'. The death was certified by the asylum's deputy medical superintendent Walter Scowcroft, who had been in charge of Briggs' welfare during his two stays in the hospital, and the certificate was also signed by the registrar, J.S.Dean. It was dated 'Thirteenth January, 1902', two days after Briggs' death.

Briggs had been in the asylum – now known as Cheadle Royal Hospital and run as a mental health care hospital by Affinity Healthcare – since the previous March. He had first been admitted there on 8 July, 1899, eight days after being taken ill with what was thought at the time to be an epileptic fit, on the evening of the first day's play in the England v Australia Test at Headingley, where he had taken three wickets in the Australian innings to bring his tally against those opponents to 97. Briggs and some of his Test-playing colleagues were enjoying themselves at a Leeds music hall when Briggs was taken ill.

Contemporary reports speculated about the cause of the illness. Some correspondents attributed it to the sheer nervousness with which he approached his recall to the England team, particularly as he was replacing Yorkshire's Wilfred Rhodes on his home ground. Rhodes was, in fact, one of five players dropped by the newly-formed selection committee from the side that had lost the previous Test at Lord's.

There was a suggestion, supported in a subsequent interview by Hornby, that the sunstroke he had suffered in South Africa in 1889 was the cause of Briggs' illness. Others put it down to an incident in a Lancashire v Surrey match at Old Trafford three weeks prior to the Headingley Test, when he had been struck a full-blooded blow under the heart by a shot from Surrey's Tom Hayward. Briggs became one of the first patients to be X-rayed – probably by a device called a fluoroscope developed four years earlier by Thomas Edison – and this examination is believed to have shown that one of Briggs' ribs had been pushed up against a heart valve. It is said that he went home that night and told his wife: 'This blow will kill me.'

Whatever the causes of his illness, it was felt that he was sufficiently recovered to be discharged seven and a half months later on 28 March, 1900. He was certainly well enough to play cricket for Lancashire again and, remarkably, take all ten wickets in Worcestershire's first innings for 55 runs at Old Trafford in May. However, his health began to deteriorate again and he was re-admitted to the asylum almost a year after his first spell in hospital, on 8 March, 1901. Later that year – some five or six weeks before his eventual demise – it was reported that he had rallied after a serious relapse, but that was the last piece of good news to come out of the hospital about Briggs' condition.

At the time of his death he was just 39 years of age. It was a tragic end to an outstanding career.

Chapter Two
Where it all began

'Very soon he succeeded in taking the Champion's wicket. The father of Briggs was told to take care of his son as he has all the qualities of making a good cricketer.' Hornsea Gazette

But the Johnny Briggs story was certainly not all doom and gloom – far from it.

He brought joy to thousands of cricket fans both in this country and abroad, mainly in Australia, where he toured six times in the days when travelling across continents was far from easy.

Briggs was a short, roly-poly figure of a man with a snub nose and a moustache which grew more luxuriant as he got older. He was only 5ft 5in tall, weighing 10st 6lb for most of his career although his weight did rise to 11st 6lb in his latter playing years, and because he was so short he was usually asked to sit cross-legged on the ground when pre-season team photographs were being taken. He was quickly given the nickname, 'Boy', which clung to him for much of his career. His physique, in fact, was a far cry from the 6ft-plus athletic cricketers of more recent years. Nevertheless, his stature and demeanour helped the ordinary spectator identify with him.

He was a brilliantly nimble fielder, mainly at cover point, and an attacking right-handed batsman who made his runs quickly before he fully developed his left-arm slow bowling style, which on the largely untreated wickets of the day produced prodigious turn both ways. He also employed the quicker ball to good effect, as a well as a high-tossed slower ball which also brought him much success.

The Briggs story began in the village of Sutton-in-Ashfield in Nottinghamshire, a county where many great English cricketers were born. (See also Appendix Two). Sutton-in-Ashfield is mentioned in the Domesday Book of 1086, being listed as a hamlet close to Mansfield. By the 1900s the population had grown to around 18,000. Briggs was born there on 3 October, 1862 almost eight hundred years after the Domesday Book appeared. His birth certificate, issued exactly a month later, records that he was the son of James and Ellen Briggs (née Banner) with the father's occupation listed as a stocking framework knitter. The informant is recorded as Ellen Briggs, mother, of Lord Street, Sutton, who placed her X in lieu of a signature on the document. Lord Street, formerly known as Bedlam Court, has subsequently been demolished to make way for Sutton Centre School.

Briggs' father, James, would have received very low pay in his job as a stocking framework knitter, which had been one of the main occupations in the village since the first hand frames for making stockings were installed in around 1770. The connection between Sutton-in-Ashfield and the hosiery industry continues to this day. James Briggs, who was on piece work, would have earned around two shillings for a dozen cotton stockings, which would usually have taken around seven hours to make. The knitters would have to work long hours to pay for the rent of the frames they used and the houses in which they lived.

So it must have been pleasing for Johnny's family when his father was able to take up a summer job as the cricket professional with the Hornsea club on the east coast of Yorkshire. Hornsea CC was founded in the mid-1860s and proved popular with players from the East Riding and Hull. It is still going strong. Back in 1871 they engaged Andrew Crossland, the former Yorkshire player, as a professional, but only for two afternoons a week because of a lack of funds. However, the club's financial position later became much healthier and it was then decided that they could afford to take on a full-time pro and in 1872 James Briggs was appointed for the year.

He remained with Hornsea for three seasons and proved a valued acquisition, the club reporting that 'by his careful attention to his duties and his abilities as a cricketer and groundsman he is held in high esteem'. James lived in Hornsea during the summer months with his wife and young Johnny, returning in the winter, presumably to take up his poorly-paid role as a stocking framework knitter.

In a three-day match, starting on 13 July, 1874, Briggs senior played for a Hornsea and District XXII against the United South of England XI, whose line-up included the greatest player of his day,

W.G.Grace. There are no reports that Briggs senior made any great contribution to this match, but it was to have great significance for Briggs junior, who was then an impressionable 11-year-old. In a report in the Hornsea Gazette in 1893, which appeared a few days after Johnny Briggs had helped win a memorable Roses match for Lancashire, the paper revealed that it was during a break in that 1874 Hornsea and District match that 'young Briggs showed to the world that he had the makings of a first-class cricketer in him'.

The article continued: 'During luncheon on one of the three days W.G.Grace came on to the ground for some practice and one of the Southern players persuaded Briggs senior to put 'Jack' (young Briggs) on bowling against the famous Gloucestershire man. After a few balls by 'Jack', the Doctor seemed a little surprised at his wonderful bowling. Very soon he succeeded in taking the Champion's wicket. The father of Briggs was told to take care of his son as he has all the qualities of making a good cricketer.'

At the end of that season James Briggs left Hornsea and although it is recorded that he did appear once against the exquisitely named touring team, the Clown Cricketers, a year later, the link with Hornsea seemed to be over as he moved first to Morley and then to Widnes, where the family lived, initially at 3 Gladstone Street in the town before moving to 30 Frederick Street. Widnes, although these days in the administrative county of Cheshire, was then part of Lancashire and the family's move meant that Briggs was able to start his residential qualification to play for Lancashire. The residential qualification rule had been brought in less than two years earlier at a meeting of the counties at The Oval on 9 June, 1873. It was a rule that one of Briggs' Old Trafford colleagues, John Crossland, would fall foul of several years later.

Although Briggs senior may have severed his ties with Hornsea, the Briggs family certainly had not, and in 1876 Hornsea took on young Briggs as a professional despite the fact that he was just 13 years old. Young Briggs was pretty candid about his abilities as a cricketer at the time and in an interview with *The Cricket Field* in 1894 he said: 'The club did not want a fully-fledged professional and they thought I might do, though I could only bowl eighteen yards. I was pretty straight but knew nothing about making the ball turn.' It must have been a lonely existence for the young cricketer who lodged in Hornsea.

He reported for his duties each day at the ground, where he provided practice for club members and didn't appear in a full-scale match until the end of June – and only then because the first eleven was a man short. He appeared in a further five games during the summer, largely as a makeweight when the numbers were low, once turning out for a team entitled the 'Eleven Lawyers', although it is not known whether the latter side had much luck with their appeals! He batted at either ten or eleven and only made runs on only two visits to the crease – he didn't bowl at all.

Briggs was re-engaged the following year and made a much improved contribution although his total tally of wickets at the season's end was only 13. However, it did include an analysis of 7 for 32 in his benefit match against a side entitled 'An XI of the Universities' although the rain-affected game raised little money for the beneficiary, something that was to be repeated on an even bigger scale later in Briggs's career. One plus point for Briggs were his figures, the sort of return for which he would later become famous.

Chapter Three
From Widnes to Old Trafford

'He was a man into whose body the humours of summer entered day by day – sunshine, wind and refreshing dews.' Neville Cardus

Briggs was not re-employed for a third season at Hornsea in the wake of a measure of disquiet among some committee members who felt that he hadn't put his whole heart and soul into the job. But, eighteen months later, Johnny Briggs was to make his first-class debut for Lancashire as a batsman/fielder.

First though, Briggs' burgeoning cricketing career took a sporting detour from their new home in Widnes, where Johnny's father had accepted the position of professional at Widnes cricket club. Remarkably, he was to continue in that role for a further 15 years until he was 51. His longevity could have been something to do with the fact that, as part of the deal, he doubled up as landlord of the Cross Keys pub in Appleton village, where James, his wife Ellen, and their six children – Johnny, Joseph Banner, James Alfred, William Harold, Sarah and Alice – set up home. Appleton, recorded

Briggs took the wicket of his older brother, Joseph Banner Briggs, when the latter played for Nottinghamshire against Lancashire at Manchester in August 1888. Briggs had Joseph Briggs, batting at No.3, caught by Watson off his bowling for four in his only innings in the match. Joseph Briggs also bowled in Lancashire's first innings, taking 0 for 21 off five overs in the match which was eventually drawn. Joseph Briggs had made his debut for Nottinghamshire in the previous month. He took 14 wickets first-class wickets at 12.00 during his short career. He died in Bramley, Leeds less than a year after Johnny Briggs, also in 1902, aged 42. Like his brother, Joseph batted right-handed and bowled slow left-arm. His best bowling analysis was 5 for 34, but he could rightly be described as a 'rabbit' as far as his batting was concerned with an average of a minuscule 2.36 from his 11 innings which brought him only 26 runs and a highest score of nine. The two brothers also played against each other at Harrogate in 1885.

as Epletune in the Domesday Book, was the township name, with Widnes being the name of the district. The population was sparse, with just a few scattered hamlets and farms in an area that was mainly marshland. Appleton still exists and is close to the centre of Widnes, which grew rapidly through its thriving chemical industry and by 1900 had a population of 50,000.

A year after Briggs senior played his first season as a pro for Widnes CC, Johnny and his older brother Joe, joined Widnes Rugby club. Just five years earlier, the forerunner to what is now known as Widnes Rugby League Football Club was formed as the Farnworth and Appleton Cricket and Football Club. Two years later the name Widnes Rugby Football Club was established, but it wasn't until 1895 that Widnes broke away from the Rugby Football Union to become founder members of the Northern Union when the new sport of Rugby League was established. Not until 1919/20, however, did Widnes claim their first honour - the Lancashire League title.

Family portrait: Briggs (standing) with his father James and brother Joseph and an unidentified cricket-playing Briggs relative

And although the club's records were poorly documented at the time of Johnny Briggs' spell at Widnes, it is safe to assume that he didn't even win minor honours with the newly-created team. Widnes, at that time, were not playing in a league system and, although of a relatively high standard, they were considered to be below the rank of top-flight rugby.

Briggs probably made his debut in Widnes colours before his sixteenth birthday, but it is known that he played in the three-quarters and his 5ft 5in frame was described as 'round but resilient'. It has been reported that his rugby career was brought to a premature end when he fractured one of the bones in his right arm after falling in a pre-match warm-up at Sale on 2 December, 1882. Several newspaper reports described this as a wake-up call to young Briggs, sending out the message to him that he ought to sacrifice his amateur, unpaid rugby career for a cricketing one that would bring much-needed cash to his hard-pressed family.

However, despite these considerations, Steve Fox, Widnes Vikings RLFC historian, says he has discovered that Briggs was still an active playing member at Widnes for three more years after his injury. In fact, he played until 5 December, 1885 when he turned out at Failsworth. Briggs had earlier been appointed captain of Widnes, but because of his cricket commitments on the 1884/85 tour to Australia, he was unable ever to take the field as Widnes skipper. Similarly, Joe Briggs was also appointed captain but never took up the role in a playing capacity either.

It was during the summer months of his sojourn at Widnes that young Briggs' cricketing career began to make real progress. In 1878, he signed for the Northern Club at Seaforth in Liverpool, a club founded 19 years earlier, and his performances marked him out as a player of promise. As a professional and at the age of 15 he was earning 35 shillings (£1.75p) a week. He did well against two of the other strong teams in the area, Anfield and Rock Ferry. Against Anfield, he scored 77 and took seven wickets, and in the return game scored 47 and captured six wickets. He followed up with 66 not out against Rock Ferry and ended the season with a batting average of 24 and more than 100 wickets at only five runs each.

He again featured for Northern in the following year, 1879, but by then had been spotted by Lancashire, playing in a benefit match for a former Lancashire professional, James Unsworth, with two

Lancashire stalwarts Richard Barlow and Alec Watson. Unsworth only played twice for Lancashire and, like other good club professionals who were employed to give amateurs practice in the nets, he found it difficult to take wickets in a competitive environment. He was given two matches by Lancashire but failed to impress and went back to club cricket, playing for Liverpool sides, Everton, Anfield, New Brighton and Huyton. The highlight of his career was his appearance for Eighteen of the Stanley Club against the Australian touring side at Stanley Park, Blackpool.

For Briggs it was a different story, with Barlow more or less taking the youngster under his wing and allowing him to lodge at his home. Writing about Briggs' performance in the benefit game in his book, 'Forty Seasons of First-Class Cricket', Barlow says: 'He [Briggs] made seven runs and showed very good form. He was also very smart in the field, his favourite place being cover-point. Briggs also bowled a little and though he did not take any wickets, we liked his delivery; in short, both Watson and I were very favourably impressed with his good all-round play.' Luckily for Lancashire, Nottinghamshire, who had wanted young Briggs to play in a Colts match for them, refused to pay his expenses from Widnes and, even though he was subsequently asked by Nottinghamshire captain Richard Daft if he would re-consider, Briggs' family turned down the approach. So Nottinghamshire's parsimony provided rich pickings for Lancashire.

Soon afterwards, on Barlow's recommendation, he was given a trial with Lancashire Colts and although not pulling up any trees, Lancashire had faith in Briggs' abilities and Barlow's judgment and, weighing in at a meagre 9st 10lb and standing just 5ft 5in tall, Briggs was to make his first-class debut in a three-day match at Trent Bridge in his native county of Nottinghamshire, starting on 26 May, 1879. At 16 years 235 days, he was the youngest player to appear for Lancashire – a record which remained with Briggs until Peter Marner made his debut for the county in 1952 against Sussex at Hove, at the age of 16 years 150 days.

Briggs top scored in Lancashire's only innings, with 36 in a total of 125, in a match that ended in a draw. His bowling performance was less auspicious with figures of 0 for 8 from four four-ball overs in Nottinghamshire's first innings and a similarly fruitless spell of 0 for 13 from six overs in the home side's second innings. In fact, Briggs was employed mainly as a fielder in those early days – he was a magnificent cover point, a position in which many great fieldsmen have made their mark. For Lancashire he was one of the early links in a very long chain of notable cover points, starting with Vernon Royle and continuing down the decades with such great fielders as Eddie Paynter, Cyril Washbrook, Bob Barber, Clive Lloyd and Graeme Fowler. Unlike the towering and predatory Lloyd, Briggs was brilliant despite his lack of size and throughout the rest of that season he was picked, in the main, for his ability to save runs in the field. He didn't play in Lancashire's second match of the season against Derbyshire at Old Trafford but did appear in the third game at home to Kent. Batting at No 6 he scored 21 as Lancashire completed an innings win. He didn't bowl in either Kent innings. In the away game against Derbyshire, he failed to score in either innings, being bowled twice and wasn't asked to turn his arm over as Lancashire completed a four-wicket win.

He wasn't selected for the Roses match against Yorkshire, nor did he play against Gloucestershire, but he was back in the side for the match against MCC at Lord's, where he was run out for ten in the first innings and suffered another duck in the second in a match MCC won by 32 runs. It was to be the final match of a fairly undistinguished first season for young Briggs, who appears to have been dropped from the championship side after Crossland and the Steel brothers, Allan and Douglas, became available at the beginning of July. It was a season when both *Lillywhite* publications, although not *Wisden,* asserted that Lancashire were joint county champions with Nottinghamshire. So Briggs, for the first time in his career, was part of a winning side. But despite his contribution, albeit a minor one, the *Wisden* of 1880 didn't appear to be sure who Briggs was, listing him first as R.Briggs for the match at Lord's and later simply referring to him as ' – Briggs'. One side-effect of his being dropped by Lancashire was that he was able to play more often for Northern and made 80 against Birkenhead Park before finally severing his connection with the Merseysiders at the end of that season.

The opening game of the following season in 1880, against MCC at Lord's, saw Briggs score 4 (run out) and 22 (second top-score) and he was back in the bowling attack although once again wicketless with 0 for 10 from five overs. He was to make 0 and 4 against Derbyshire and 13 and another 0 against Nottinghamshire. However, in the game against Yorkshire at Bramall Lane, Sheffield, he produced a remarkable bowling analysis of 11-10-4-0, proving his ability to pin batsmen down when given the opportunity. With

Lancashire's bowling attack one of the strongest in the land, it was disappointing for Briggs, but hardly surprising that he was never handed the ball again during that second season, although he was twice second-top scorer in an innings – in that match against Yorkshire (25) and against W.G.Grace's Gloucestershire (31 not out). In the second innings of the latter match he was bowled by the great man himself for a useful 15.

But 1880 did provide two minor milestones in Briggs' career – his first first-class wicket and his first representative honour. Both landmarks were reached in a low-key fixture, not even covered by *Wisden*, with Briggs, although a professional, playing in a three-day match for the Gentlemen of the North against the Players of the North at Manchester, starting on 29 July. Opening the attack with his Lancashire colleague Vernon Royle, Briggs bowled very economically, taking 4 for 39 in the first innings. He did even better second time around, when he took the new ball with Nottinghamshire's Joseph Sulley, finishing with 5 for 34. His breakthrough first wicket was Thomas Foster, the experienced Derbyshire professional, batting at No.5 for the Players. He was caught by the 19-year-old Sydney Evershed in the outfield. Evershed, from the famous Burton brewing family, was later to captain Derbyshire.

Cricketing prodigy:
Briggs in his early days

In 1881, Briggs, now 18, finally established himself as a regular in the Lancashire ranks, playing in all 13 of the club's matches against other counties and in the fixtures against MCC and Cambridge University. Under Hornby's captaincy, the side won ten of its county matches and this time even *Wisden* recognised their right to be called outright county champions. But with Barlow, Crossland, Nash and Watson in the ascendancy, Briggs was afforded just four overs and two of these were in the opening match of the season against MCC at Lord's when he took two wickets without conceding a run, his first for the county. But it was his batting which took the eye of one of *Wisden*'s contributors, who recorded that in that match at Lord's on a wet pitch Lancashire's success was 'due to the excellent batting of Briggs who played the bowling of Shaw, Morley and Barnes with ease and determination'. But, still they gave him the initial 'R' in the scorecard!

The 1882 season was another which sparked a debate about who had actually won the county championship. *Cricket* magazine and *Wisden* were in the Lancashire camp, but the *Lillywhite* publications begged to differ, opining that the honour should be shared by the Old Trafford club and Nottinghamshire as it had been in 1880. Whatever the merits of the respective arguments, there was no doubt that Lancashire had had another successful season, winning 12 of their 16 county games, but Briggs' contribution was well below average. Playing in 20 first-class matches altogether, including one for a Liverpool and District side, Briggs scored only 287 runs at an average of 10.25 and took only six wickets in 77.2 four-ball overs at 21.16 each.

To some, it seemed that Briggs' 'apprenticeship' was taking rather longer than had been anticipated. It was almost certainly the lowest point in his career and there may well have been some on the Lancashire committee who were even questioning whether it would be worthwhile extending his contract for a further year. Briggs had started the 1882 season bowling in both innings against MCC at Lord's, taking 1 for 20 in the second. He followed up his Lord's efforts with 4 for 11 in 5.2 overs against Cambridge University at Fenner's, but thereafter bowled rarely, largely because of the prior claims of senior professionals. However, he did manage to claim his first inter-county victim against Kent at Maidstone in mid-August when he had Lord Harris – a man who was later to have a big impact on Briggs' bowling career – caught

Liverpool and District played fourteen first-class matches at Aigburth from 1882 to 1894. Briggs played in two of these, in 1882 and 1884, but with mediocre results to the say the least. He mustered only 40 runs in four innings for an average of 13.33 with a highest score of 23 and recorded bowling figures of 0 for 31. Other Lancashire players who appeared in first-class fixtures for the team included two men who captained the county, Sydney Crosfield and Archie MacLaren, as well as Dick Pilling, Richard Barlow and Allan Steel.

and bowled. Just prior to that, Briggs' 30 against Somerset helped set up an innings win at Old Trafford. But his performance was completely overshadowed by Nash – a slow left-armer like Briggs – who took four wickets in four balls and had final figures of 4 for 14 as the home side completed an innings victory, bowling the visitors out for 29 and 51. Denied a chance with the ball, Briggs was to end the year struggling with the bat, appearing on the scorecard at either No.8 or 9, and a thoroughly unhappy season drew to a close with him being left out of the side for the final match against Middlesex at Old Trafford.

In the 1883 season Lancashire's title challenge faltered after they had won their first four games and they won only another two of their remaining eight fixtures. But Briggs had begun to turn his career around and was building quite a reputation as a batsman. He had been returned to his position in the middle order and scored his first half century (55) against Derbyshire, an innings which *Wisden* described as 'faultless', following up with further fifties against Oxford University (52) and in the return match with Derbyshire (60), his highest first-class score thus far. The latter innings also drew praise from *Wisden* which described his half century as 'very freely hit'. The latter match, which Lancashire won by an innings, was notable for the performances of Barlow and Watson, who bowled unchanged in both Derbyshire innings, taking 18 wickets between them. It might well have been all 20 but for Derbyshire's George Hay being absent hurt in both innings. But as far as Briggs' bowling was concerned, he once again had limited opportunities, taking just a single wicket for 89 runs in the championship. It must have been a little frustrating for Briggs, who after all at the tender age of 11, was bowling to the legendary W.G.Grace, to see his progress once again being blocked by the established quartet of Barlow, Crossland, Nash and Watson. *Wisden* didn't mince words, describing his 1883 bowling efforts as 'a complete failure'.

Briggs played in two end-of-season exhibition matches in Yorkshire – at Holbeck and Batley – for R.G.Barlow's XI, which involved many of the more successful Northern and Midlands professionals of the day. It was recognition from his peers that he belonged alongside them as one of the leading paid players in the game. Those games brought the curtain down on Briggs' 1883 campaign, but for the Lancashire committee, no doubt smarting at their failure to retain the title, there was a sting in the tail when

Nottinghamshire informed them that they would not renew their fixtures with Lancashire because they believed that Crossland had broken his residential qualification for Lancashire.

During the following campaign in 1884, Lancashire's headquarters at Old Trafford became a Test venue for the first time – four years after The Oval but 11 days before Lord's – although at county level they fell behind their adversaries Nottinghamshire. Briggs started the season well with his then highest score of 74, including 12 fours, against an MCC side, including W.G.Grace, at Lord's. *Wisden* reported that Briggs had batted with 'great freedom'. He also took two wickets and pouched two catches, but his exploits failed to stop Lancashire succumbing to an innings defeat. In the next match, against Derbyshire at Old Trafford, Briggs was to score his maiden first-class century, 112, batting at No.6. Again *Wisden* was full of praise for Briggs, remarking on his 'brilliant hitting'. This time his good work wasn't wasted and the home side secured a 42-run victory.

Later in the year, he scored 75 not out in the Roses match against Yorkshire at Bramall Lane, Sheffield in a six-wicket win for the visitors. He ended the season with a highly respectable run total of 667, albeit at an average of 19.61 and took 15 catches. But, more to the point, with Nash out of the Lancashire side for most of the season and Crossland missing in August, he was called into the attack in 16 matches and was rewarded with 17 wickets at 25.23 with career-best figures of 6 for 54, bowling unchanged with Watson (Barlow was playing against Australia) as Somerset were bowled out for 86 in an eight-wicket win for Lancashire. In a satisfying end to the match, Briggs was at the crease on ten not out when the winning runs were struck.

During the season, Briggs played in five 'representative' matches of varying quality, including four times when the Australian touring side provided the opposition. Against the Australians, he appeared twice for the Players (at Sheffield and The Oval); once for an England XI (at Aston Lower Grounds, Birmingham, one of only two first-class matches ever played at this venue) and once for the North of England (at Old Trafford). He also played for the Players against the Gentlemen at The Oval. It was a clear sign that he was now considered more than just a run-of-the-mill county pro although, in truth, his contribution with both bat and ball was modest to say the least. Four times he lost his wicket to Australia's Fred 'The Demon' Spofforth and he bowled only a few token overs.

Interestingly, Briggs kept up his poor record against Spofforth when appearing for Liverpool and District against Australia at Aigburth, succumbing once again to the Australian fast bowler in the first innings of a match that the visitors won by one wicket.

Briggs had a good record in matches for the Players against the Gentlemen, scoring 420 runs (at 19.09) and taking 56 wickets (at 17.60 apiece). The Gentlemen-Players fixture was one of the oldest series in cricket and began in 1806. It was normally played at Lord's although other venues, including The Oval and Scarborough, were used from time to time. Other grounds on which the match has been played included Blackpool, Hove, Hastings, Folkestone, Bournemouth and the Prince's Ground in west London.

Chapter Four
Touring Australia for the first time

'Why, he beams on you before and after your innings. The shorter your innings, the happier he is towards you.' C.B.Fry

Briggs was a late – and surprise –choice for Alfred Shaw and Arthur Shrewsbury's XI for the 1884/85 tour of Australia, when a number of more experienced players declined Shaw and Shrewsbury's terms. In those days tours were run on a purely commercial basis – national selectors were not appointed until 1899. Briggs was the only Lancashire man among the twelve players, all of them Northern professionals, together with James Lillywhite junior, who umpired and took the field in a number of minor matches. There were no amateurs in the party, with the organisers believing that their claims for expenses would endanger the tour's potential profitability. Notwithstanding the machinations over money, it was a major step forward for Briggs, who had not even been a remote possibility for the England side which Lancashire had chosen for the inaugural Old Trafford Test against Australia in July, 1884. Yorkshire's Ted Peate, who in his early days was part of the touring Clown Cricketers side against whom Briggs' father James had once appeared, had played for England in that match, while Peel went to Australia as the main slow left-armer.

Now Briggs was on his way to Australia to play against a Combined Australia side and was determined to make the best of this golden opportunity. The tourists travelled on the *SS Orient*, leaving Plymouth on their long journey on 19 September and arriving at Port Adelaide early on the morning of 29 October, going on by train to Adelaide. They had had an unusually calm run through the Bay of Biscay and were able to disembark at Port Said where they played an odds match – where the teams were uneven both in numbers and ability – against a combined Army and Navy side on a matting wicket. It was obviously a difficult surface, England making 117 while the Army and Navy XXII were precariously placed at 40 for 11 at the close of the one-day game. Later some of the players were able avail themselves of a sightseeing tour of

Cairo and the Pyramids in the company of man whose name has subsequently become a byword for travel, Thomas Cook. The latter had come to Egypt to see the Khedive, who was at that time the governor and monarch of Egypt, with the country still under Ottoman rule. Cook was trying to arrange tours up the Nile for his then fledgling travel company. The scheduled stop at Naples had been cancelled because of an outbreak of cholera in the port city.

The *SS Orient* was owned by the Orient Steam Navigation Company and was completed in 1879. Constructed of iron with two funnels and four masts, which were rigged for sail, she was at the time – 5 June, 1879 – the largest steamer to have rolled off the slipway at the Clyde shipyard, where she had been built by John Elder of Glasgow. Five months later the 5,386-ton vessel set off from London on her maiden voyage to Melbourne and Sydney via the Cape of Good Hope, returning through the Suez Canal. The Orient could accommodate 120 first-class, 130 second-class and 300 steerage class passengers. She could carry 1,500 when transformed into a troop ship during the Boer War five years after she had transported Briggs and his colleagues to and from Australia. Briggs was making his first trip abroad when he set sail on board the Orient and was reported to have suffered badly from sea-sickness during the 41-day voyage.

The driving forces behind the tour – Shaw, Shrewsbury and Lillywhite, respectively team manager, captain and umpire – had relied heavily on John Conway, who was that rare and dangerous combination of fast bowler and journalist. Conway, who lived in Victoria and organised most of the itinerary and fixtures, was a reliable 'agent', having set up previous tours. With so few in the tour party and with Shaw having to return to England in February

> Briggs was accident-prone. In addition to breaking an arm playing rugby for Widnes, he also cut his eyebrow playing hockey and crashed into a tram while cycling home from Old Trafford. He also sprained his right ankle when called for a quick single by Hornby in a match against Yorkshire and was out of action for several weeks. In Australia it is well documented that his pipe rammed into the roof of his mouth when a horse unseated him. In another equestrian incident in Australia he was thrown when dismounting and almost flung over the edge of a precipice. He was also struck under the heart by a blow from Surrey batsman Tom Hayward in a match at Old Trafford three weeks before the fateful Headingley Test.

after playing only eight times, every player appeared in virtually every game, although Briggs missed out on one of the odds fixtures, against Armidale XXII in northern New South Wales on 2 March because of injury. He didn't play in either of the two matches which followed that fixture, with Lillywhite standing in for him in the games at Ashfield, also in New South Wales, and Wellington in South Australia. At one stage, English professionals Robert Henderson, of Surrey and George Hearne, an MCC ground bowler, who were already in Australia, were co-opted into the side for three matches, as injuries from the uneven outfields and poor pitches began to mount up. The tour was certainly no sinecure with 33 matches played on Australian soil and one at Port Said over the course of a punishing 84 playing days – sometimes in wintry weather, other times in almost unbearable heat. In one game the post-lunch restart was delayed because of the high temperature.

Eight of these matches, the only eleven-a-side games they played, were treated as first-class by the press and later by statisticians: the arrangements were that these would be played to a finish in accordance with the established local custom. Five of them, against the Combined Australian XI – Australia then comprised of separate colonies – were treated as international matches of importance and later canonised as Test matches. Three other matches played eleven-a-side were against New South Wales and Victoria. Twenty five matches, mostly limited to two days, were played against odds – fifteens, eighteens and twenty-twos – most of them in country towns away from the colonial capitals.

To fulfil this fixture list, which involved matches in four colonies – South Australia, Victoria, New South Wales and Queensland – Shaw and Shrewsbury's caravan zig-zagged over much of the inhabited eastern half of Australia, stopping in hotels of variable quality and travelling as far north as Maryborough in Queensland, more than 100 miles beyond Brisbane. The journeys between matches were made by train, horse-drawn road vehicles and coastal steamships, and totalled in excess of 8,000 miles, with some fixtures almost 500 miles apart. The batting surfaces were as varied as their modes of transport with the tourists encountering matting, concrete, bare earth and turf pitches which differed greatly in quality and preparation.

A combination of fatigue, minor injuries and sheer weight of numbers meant that Shaw and Shrewsbury's team won only ten of its 25 odds matches – often they simply found it beyond them to dismiss for a second time the seemingly never-ending stream of local batsmen paraded before them. But Briggs was clearly enjoying himself – as one would expect from a 22-year-old on his first trip abroad playing the game he loved – and on his return from the tour he was thought of as a fully-fledged international cricketer. *Wisden*'s comment that 'his dashing play fully warranted his inclusion in the team' only served to enhance his standing.

In the odds matches, Peel took 321 wickets at 4.22 with William Attewell, Barnes and Wilfred Flowers accounting for most of the other 450 wickets. Briggs bowled in only three matches taking 5 for 62 in 50 four-ball overs. As a batsman he scored 627 runs in 27 innings at an average of 25.08 and only three batsmen scored more in these matches. His highest score was 98 not out off what was described as 'worn out bowling'. Briggs, never one to look a gift horse in the mouth, took full advantage of the poor quality of the opposition hitting six fives against Bendigo XVIII at Sandhurst, Victoria on Christmas Eve, when Shaw's XI scored 576 for 6 declared, before dismissing their snail-like opposition for a tedious 82 in 81.2 overs. The first tour fixture began just two days after the party had disembarked at Port Adelaide and the visitors had little time to shake off their 'sea legs' before they were taking the field against XV of Adelaide. They got off to a winning start with a three-wicket success although they were far from impressive. There followed matches against XVIII of South Australia, Victoria at Melbourne, New South Wales at Sydney, XXII of Hawkesbury, XVIII of Cumberland and XXII of Clarence River before the first Test. Briggs played in the timeless match for Alfred Shaw's XI against New South Wales at Sydney. Batting at eight, he had an inauspicious match, scoring 0 and 0 not out. Quite clearly it wasn't his finest hour on a cricket field although Shaw's team pulled off a four-wicket win.

In the four-day match against Victoria at the Melbourne Cricket Ground, which began on 14 November, 1884, Briggs, again batting at No.8 for Shaw's XI in both innings, made 33 (third highest score in the innings) and five. He had not established himself as a bowler, even in the Lancashire side, and was not called upon to turn his arm over.

Briggs made his Test debut at the Adelaide Oval, where the side included Peel, also appearing in his first Test. Peel made a much more auspicious first appearance for England than his fellow debutant, taking eight wickets, while Briggs, reported as 'far from well', hardly made a contribution to England's eight-wicket win, scoring one run, coming in at No.8 again and not bowling, despite the fact that England employed six bowlers in each Australian innings.

The rivalry between Briggs and Peel, at 5ft 6in just an inch taller than Briggs, continued over many years with the pair touring Australia together on four occasions in an era when playing two left-arm spinners in the same starting eleven was not considered unusual. The pair were closely matched and Grace could never forecast which of the duo was likely to fare best. In his book, *Cricketing Reminiscences and Recollections,* first published in 1899, the doctor wrote: 'On apparently similar wickets Peel would fail when Johnny was doing brilliantly, while on another day Peel would carry everything before him when Johnny could do nothing. The why and wherefore of it all were a puzzle to me, as it happened not once but many times and I could never determine which was the right man to put on bowling, as both seemed to bowl equally well, but with fluctuating results.' But it wasn't Briggs' bowling that was to make the headlines in the sporting pages in the Second Test, which began at Melbourne on New Year's Day. He had been moved up the order to No.7 and responded by scoring a magnificent 121, occupying the crease for only 150 minutes and striking 15 fours. It remained Briggs' highest score in a Test. He was 65 not out overnight after England, having won the toss and elected to bat, had reached 303 for 9 at the close. On the next day Briggs, together with the Yorkshire wicket-keeper Joseph Hunter, who was 39 not out, marshalled the side to a formidable all-out total of 401, the pair putting on an extremely valuable 98 for the final wicket.

Briggs had come to the crease on day one with England on 194 for 5, but it wasn't long before he lost his initial partner, J.M.Read, bowled off his legs by Sam Jones with England on 204 for 6. Next ball, Ulyett was clean bowled by Jones with England now seven wickets down. Attewell had now joined Briggs in the middle and it looked as though the Australians were right back in the game. But Attewell and Briggs, by dint of some clean hitting, added a useful 50 before Attewell was caught by Jones off Jack Worrall. Peel was next man in and Briggs took charge as the pair advanced the score by 49, with Peel's contribution only five before he was clean bowled by Jones and play ended for the day.

Day two began in bright sunshine at 12.15pm with Briggs and his new partner, Hunter, moving purposefully to the wicket. Australia, needing just one wicket to wrap up the England innings, must have felt they would be soon be taking advantage of what appeared to be ideal batting conditions. But Briggs and Hunter took the fight to the home side, the latter twice driving Bruce to the boundary to set the tempo with Briggs adding a further eight fours.

The Australians rang the changes to their bowling attack, but it made little difference as Briggs sailed on to his century. After reaching three figures his concentration must have dipped a little as he offered chances at 104 (missed at mid-off) and 117 (put down at short slip) before being brilliantly caught at square leg by the home captain, Tom Horan, off the bowling of the reliable Jones. *Wisden* described Horan's tumbling effort as one of the best ever witnessed at the ground. The pair had added 98 runs in an hour as they advanced the total to 401. Briggs might well have been the recipient of one of the earliest 'Man of the Match' awards in cricket history, being presented with a prize of £10 by a cricket supporter for his efforts at the crease. More to the point, he was even cheered off the field by the home crowd.

It is fair to say that Briggs' achievement must be tempered by the fact that the Australians fielded a shadow team, with nine players making their Test debuts after those who had represented Australia in the First Test demanded 50 per cent of the gate receipts as their match fee for the Second Test. Unsurprisingly, the Australian Cricket Association declined to do business on these terms and, of the eleven which took the field at the MCG, only two – Horan and Jones – had played at this level before. One of the players making his debut was Sam Morris, born in Hobart of West Indian parents, who thus became the first non-white to represent Australia.

After compiling his hundred, Briggs even got to bowl for the first time in a Test, but his eight four-ball overs produced no wickets although his spell cost him only 13 runs - a fair performance as he had been hampered by an injury in the field which had split his little finger. But although Australia's scratch team battled hard, England romped to a ten-wicket win, needing just five for victory in their second innings.

Briggs came down to earth with a bump in the match against New South Wales which followed the Second Test despite again being moved up the order to No.6, scoring a solitary run before being bowled. Despite Briggs' lack of success, Shaw's XI won easily, by an innings and 37 runs. Briggs did not have a good Third Test at Sydney. He scored one in the first innings and contributed only three to England's chase for 214 in the second, the side ultimately falling short by just seven runs as Australia, in a thrilling finish, pulled back the series deficit to 1-2.

The Fourth Test, also played at Sydney, was marginally better for Briggs, but he must still have been bitterly disappointed with his performance, scoring three and five as Australia sauntered home by eight wickets to level the series.

It was back to Melbourne for the series decider and here Briggs made a useful 43 in England's first innings total of 386, a score which was enough to see England home to an innings success and a 3-2 win in the series.

On the return journey, several players left the ship, the Orient Line's *SS Potosi*, at Naples – this had been common practice on other tours – and reached England overland by rail on 12 May. Briggs and five other players remained on board as the ship returned via Gibraltar. The six remaining members of the party finally disembarked at Plymouth on 15 May. But there was little rest for Briggs – just six days later he was in action for Lancashire against Oxford University at The Parks. He batted in both innings, but wasn't asked to bowl.

Chapter Five
Coming of age as a cricketer

'One has known dull days and dull cricket before the advent of Briggs, but he had just to show his face and a light passed over the field, and with it companionable warmth.' Neville Cardus

After his experiences on tour, the 1885 season saw a further improvement in Briggs' batting average which had climbed to 27.64, with two centuries and two fifties for Lancashire. He achieved his highest score (186) against Surrey at Liverpool – a total he never bettered in his career – and ended the season with the second highest Lancashire aggregate of runs (578), beaten only by the bearded Richard Barlow, who totalled 698 for an average just in excess of 30.

Bolton-born Barlow, later immortalised along with Hornby, in the poem 'At Lord's' by Francis Thompson, which ended with the line, 'Oh my Hornby and my Barlow long ago', played 17 Tests for England, scoring 591 runs and taking 34 wickets. He was the first great Lancashire professional, spending 21 seasons at Old Trafford, amassing 11,217 runs (average 20.61) and taking 951 wickets (at 14.50). He was a dogged opener and scored the then slowest half century in county cricket against Kent at Maidstone in 1889, taking 290 minutes to reach 50. In his innings of five not out against Nottinghamshire at Trent Bridge, Barlow remained scoreless for 80 minutes. Always a difficult man to dislodge, he carried his bat through an innings on no fewer than 11 occasions. He was also more than useful with the ball in hand, achieving the hat-trick three times for Lancashire and once for the Players versus the Gentlemen at The Oval in 1884. Barlow is also responsible for the saying 'I take my hat off to you' becoming part of the language. It happened in 1884 when the North of England played the Australians on a poor wicket at Trent Bridge. Barlow, who had opened the batting and bowling at both county and Test level, had a marvellous all-round match, scoring a century and taking 10 wickets.

Billy Murdoch, the Australian captain, was so impressed with Barlow's performance that he approached him as he left the field and said those immortal words 'I take my cap off to you' which later became 'I take my hat off to you'. Although he left school at 14, Barlow was a talented and inventive man and designed wicket covers, removable cricket spikes, the single-strap leg-guard, an air-tight valve and a laceless football. Unfortunately, his covers were by no means in universal use – not even at Old Trafford. Barlow lamented after the 1890 Test in Manchester, where not a single ball was bowled because of the inclement weather: 'Much of this disappointment might have been avoided if my patent wicket protector had been used.' He played football to county level and later became a referee, officiating at a match that has been etched into soccer folklore – the FA Cup first round tie between Preston North End and Hyde FC at Deepdale in October 1887 which ended in a record 26-0 win for Preston. Barlow wrote later in his reminiscences: 'I may say that had the Hyde goalkeeper not been in good form, North End would have materially increased their score. I have never seen such splendid shooting and passing in my life.' Barlow also umpired at first-class level for 21 years, including one Test match. Thirty two years after refereeing that famous FA Cup tie, Barlow died at the age of 68. He was buried at Stanley Park cemetery, Blackpool, not far from one of Lancashire's most popular 'out grounds'.

It was in 1885, now 23 but still looking more like a boy than a man, that Briggs came of age as a cricketer, playing at representative level as a batsman and proving his worth for Lancashire as a bowler. Prior to that season, Lancashire had relied on Barlow, Watson, Nash and Crossland as their main bowling attack. But both Nash and Crossland were under scrutiny over their allegedly suspect actions and the latter was also dogged by questions over whether he was residentially qualified to play for Lancashire. In fact, Nash and Crossland had both played in Lancashire's first two matches of the season – against Oxford University in a twelve-a-side game, and against Kent. Crossland, like Briggs, came from Sutton-in-Ashfield, and regularly returned to the county of his birth to work as a coal miner. Despite this residential discrepancy, Lancashire continued to field Crossland, ignoring objections from several counties.

But it was Nottinghamshire, closely matched with Lancashire in the fight for the championship in the previous four seasons, who brought matters to a head. They claimed, irrespective of the legitimacy of Crossland's bowling action, and it must be remembered he had played for them in non-first-class matches, that he was not eligible on grounds of residential qualification. The two counties even exchanged acrimonious greetings cards on the subject one winter with Lancashire sending a Christmas card to Trent Bridge, which included the line that Lancashire batsman 'shall not be allowed to use bats, but only broom handles' when playing against Nottinghamshire. Soon a New Year's card was on its way from Nottingham to Manchester, which suggested that Lancashire would only field in their county eleven, players 'that shall neither have been born in, nor reside in, Lancashire'.

There were even more rancorous exchanges on the matter, fully reported in *Wisden*, after Lancashire had beaten Kent at Manchester on 28-30 May. The Kent captain, Lord Harris, wrote a long letter to the Lancashire committee, outlining his objections to the bowling actions of Nash and Crossland, and reminding Lancashire that they had declined to follow the lead of other counties in agreeing not to employ bowlers with suspect actions. Lancashire made a vigorous defence of their two bowlers, sending copies of the correspondence to Lord's and pointing out that MCC had chosen Crossland to play in the annual North versus South match, thereby implying Lord's was satisfied with his action. Crossland had, in fact, devastated the South batting in this match, taking seven wickets in each innings although he couldn't prevent a southern victory.

The upshot of Lancashire's reply to Lord Harris's criticism was that the Kent secretary wrote to his Lancashire counterpart stating that Kent had cancelled the return match which was to have been played at Tonbridge in the following August.

In the event, Lancashire did not select Nash for a first-class game after the fixture against Kent, citing the dry, hard pitches. He ended up playing for Darlington. In the case of Crossland, Nottinghamshire complained to MCC under Rule IV of the regulations concerning qualifications, claiming that he had failed to maintain proper residence in Lancashire. In its first adverse decision under these regulations, MCC upheld Nottinghamshire's complaint and disqualified the player in the last week of June. He played his final game for the county against Sussex at Hove on 22-24 June, bowing out in rather sad fashion, bagging a pair and bowling only nine four-ball overs for no wickets. He made his last appearance for Lancashire in a non-championship match against Cheshire at Stockport in the same month. After that he disappeared from the county scene and ended up playing club cricket locally, turning out for East Lancashire, Church and Colne. Out of the Lancashire side, Crossland didn't play at first-class level again for Nottinghamshire either. Not that they needed him: they had the best bowling line-up in the championship and were awarded the title by the unanimous vote of all the relevant cricket journals.

Cue Briggs stage right – and he was quick to seize the opportunity presented to him by Lancashire's loss of two of their front-line bowlers. After all, he had been waiting in the wings long enough. Soon he was showing what *Wisden* was to describe as 'a capacity for bowling of the highest order'. His bowling career never looked back. Against Oxford University in mid-June, he gave his colleagues – and Lancashire's supporters – a taste of what was to become standard fare, taking eleven wickets, scattering the lower order in both innings. He took eight wickets in the match against Sussex at Hove; twelve against MCC at Lord's in July and 9 for 29 in 42 overs, the best return of his career to date, in Derbyshire's second innings on a drying pitch in blustery conditions at Derby in the first week of August. He consolidated his reputation with 15 for 57 in a minor two-day match against Cheshire and 6 for 34 in the second innings of a similar fixture against Essex at Leyton. In Lancashire's final two first-class matches of the season, he opened the bowling with Watson and took five in an innings against both Gloucestershire and Surrey.

His overall return for the season in all first-class cricket was 67 wickets at an average of 13.74, which put him ahead of any other regularly performing bowler in the land, with eight five-wickets-in-an-innings hauls. In Lancashire's last eight county matches, he took 44 wickets. In the preceding 54 county matches in which he had played, Briggs had taken only 15 wickets. Put simply, Briggs had arrived as a bowler.

Although neither Nash nor Crossland were ever called for throwing, that fate did befall a colleague of Briggs in this season. George Jowett, an amateur from Prescot playing in his first match, against Surrey at Liverpool, was no-balled by umpire John Platts in one of his two four-ball overs in the visitors' second innings. Jowett, who played mainly as a batsman in nineteen matches for the Red Rose county, appears to have been brought in as a fast bowler at this early point in his career. However, he bowled only 100 deliveries, taking no wickets for 55 in his four seasons of first-class cricket between 1885 and 1889. He played in no first-class matches in 1886.

It was in Jowett's debut match against Surrey that Briggs hit the highest score of his career – 186 – just two days after his wedding. It was, according to contemporary reports, 'a rare exhibition of hard and clean hitting' and was notable in one other respect, a partnership of 173 in only 100 minutes for the last wicket with wicket-keeper Dick Pilling, which was at the time a record for first-class cricket and stands to this day as a Lancashire record. It took the introduction of Walter Read, whose mixture of lobs and round-arm deliveries brought him 100 first-class wickets in a 25-year career, before the partnership was severed with the stumping of Briggs off a Read lob. Briggs and Pilling shared a collection round the ground of £28 8s 4d (£28.42p). However, the Briggs-Pilling partnership didn't produce a victory for the home side. Surrey – thanks to the loss of the final day of three – were able to escape with a draw. Hornby remarked: 'I'd be married every day if I could bat as Briggs has done.' The newspapers dubbed the game 'the honeymoon match'.

The Briggs-Pilling partnership easily surpassed the pervious highest stand for the last wicket of 128 between William Mudie and Tom Sewell jun for Surrey against Kent and Sussex at The Oval in 1859 before overarm bowling was legalised. It remained the highest ever tenth wicket stand for the last wicket until Richard Nicholls and William Roche for Middlesex against Kent at Lord's in 1899. The pair took Middlesex from a perilous 55 for 9 to the relative riches of 285 all out, helping their side to an 118-run win. However, it is the oldest surviving county partnership record for any wicket, apart from the one involving W.G.Grace and William Moberley for Gloucestershire, which was set in 1876. The pair added 261 for the fifth wicket in the first innings against Yorkshire at Cheltenham.

Apart from county matches in 1885, Briggs played in three of the four most important representative fixtures of the season, games which took on an even greater significance because of the fact that there was no touring team in England that year. He played, as a middle order batsman, for the North against the South on his home ground, scoring 52 in each innings, and for the Players in their two mid-season games in London against the Gentlemen. In the first of them, at The Oval, Briggs scored 85 in the first innings, while in the second game, Briggs was making his first appearance at Lord's in this prestigious match. His invitation to take part in these fixtures was an indication of his growing prominence in the game. However, he did not play in the end-of-season Gentlemen versus Players match at the Scarborough Festival, where *Wisden* suggests his place was rather unsurprisingly taken by local favourite Tom Emmett, of Yorkshire.

In the following season – 1886 – normal service was resumed as far as Lancashire, Nottinghamshire and Kent were concerned, thus expanding the Lancashire fixture list against other counties to fourteen. Briggs played in all these matches, three other games for Lancashire, nine times against the Australian tourists, including three Tests, and for the Players against the Gentlemen at Lord's. With 27 matches under his belt, it was his busiest first-class season so far.

Lancashire did not make much of a fist of their championship challenge, but Briggs, becoming ever more popular among the knowledgeable crowds which followed the game, was in demand for representative and privately-raised sides of all hues, including at the Scarborough Festival. In total he collected 92 victims at 15.96, his best aggregate so far, although his batting dropped away a little with 722 runs at 19.51. From mid-season onwards he was

> Briggs played in several Lancashire matches that were completed in a single day, including matches against MCC at Lord's in 1886, against Surrey at Old Trafford in 1888, against Somerset at Old Trafford in 1892) and again against Somerset at Old Trafford in 1894.

often entrusted with opening the bowling. He remained in the middle order for Lancashire, but batted lower down the card in representative games.

But in the midst of this marvellous season, there was a mysterious incident when Briggs inexplicably went 'missing' for two days without permission. The committee, not best pleased by Briggs' absence, deducted two days' wages from him, but no one knew where he had gone or what he was doing. Some have speculated that he had suffered an epileptic fit, but there is no evidence, anecdotal or otherwise, for this assertion.

In the home Tests against Australia, much to the disappointment of the crowd, Briggs did next to nothing in the opening match of the three-game series on his home ground at Old Trafford, which England won by four wickets. He failed to shine with the bat and wasn't called upon to bowl.

But his career underwent a sea change in the Second Test at Lord's when he was quite clearly England's match-winner with the ball, taking 5 for 29 and 6 for 45 as England romped to an innings and 106-run victory. It hadn't looked promising for England until captain Allan Steel, himself a Lancastrian and a colleague of Briggs at Old Trafford, called on Briggs as first change with Australia 45 for 1. Briggs didn't let Steel down and Australia were all out for only 121 with Briggs' figures 34-22-29-5. When the Australians followed on, Briggs rattled through them again. His reputation as an international bowler was firmly established that day. For Steel, although not a regular captain, it was another success. He had an uncanny knack of getting the best out of teams under his command and gained notable wins for Marlborough over Rugby, Gentleman against Players, Cambridge against Oxford, Lancashire versus Yorkshire, and of course, England against their deadly foes, Australia. An outstanding all-rounder, Steel was rated second only to Grace by his peers.

In the final Test, at The Oval, Briggs continued his good form, making 53 and taking 3 for 28 and 3 for 30 as the home side completed another massive win, this time by an innings and 217 runs.

Briggs was touring once again in 1886/87 with Shaw's XI down under, leaving Plymouth on board the Orient liner *Cuzco* on 18 September, and arriving in Adelaide on 29 October, with a ten-hour stopover in Aden. His Lancashire colleague Barlow was also in the party, having previously toured with Shaw and Shrewsbury's team in 1881/82 and the Hon Ivo Bligh's team in 1882/83. The Indian Ocean leg was distinctly choppy and Briggs, just as he had on his first tour, suffered from sea sickness along with William Gunn (who later founded the successful sports firm, Gunn and Moore), Barlow, Lillywhite and Billy Bates. The latter's career was cut short a year later when he was hit in the face by a ball in the nets while on a non-Test tour of Australia led by George Vernon. The injury damaged his sight to such an extent that he was never able to play at first-class level again. He became so depressed by the injury that at one point he attempted suicide. However, Huddersfield-born

Bates, who played eleven seasons for Yorkshire, died of natural causes after catching a cold at the funeral of a fellow Yorkshire player, John Thewlis. In the days after the funeral, Bates' condition worsened and he passed away. He was 45.

The tourists whiled away the long hours on board ship with games of deck cricket, whist drives, concerts and a fancy-dress ball as well as other sporting entertainments. Briggs won a potato race, finished second in a hopping race and gained another second place, together with the Nottinghamshire left-hander William Scotton, in the three-legged race.

This tour was run, once again, as a commercial enterprise under the stewardship of Shaw, Shrewsbury and Lillywhite, but it was neither as profitable nor as arduous as the previous tour in which Briggs had participated. However, in terms of quality of players it gained greater recognition. *Wisden* described the side as 'one of the strongest that ever left England for the colonies' which underlines the position Briggs had attained in the game in 1885 and 1886. On the travelling side, the tourists were spared their previous excursion to Queensland which chopped many miles off their itinerary. But there was still plenty of cricket to be played with a total of 29 matches, ten of which were deemed to be first-class and they still had the likes of the twenty-twos of Cootamundra, Bowral and Ballarat with which to contend. As a consequence the 13-strong playing party was fully stretched over 76 days of cricketing action, leaving little room for manoeuvre in terms of illness and injury. The normally injury-prone Briggs seems to have escaped unscathed from this tour, but Billy Barnes wasn't so lucky. He was hurt in a fight, which resulted in the little-known Reginald Wood, a public schoolboy seemingly down on his luck, being co-opted into the touring party for three matches, including one Test. Wood, from Birkenhead, had played alongside Briggs for Lancashire between 1880 and 1884. He played for Birkenhead Park and for Liverpool and District, emigrating to Australia in 1885. He later became a professional coach at East Melbourne CC and later at Melbourne CC and at the Albert club in Sydney.

On the 1886/87 tour, Shaw's side played many warm-up matches prior to the initial Test and Briggs had had two five-wicket hauls (against New South Wales and in the first of two matches against an Australian XI) and had scored a useful 69 in the second match against an Australian XI. In contrast to his previous tour, Briggs was being played mainly as a bowler and he had been relegated to No.8 or 9 in the batting order in first-class matches. However, in the Tests themselves, Briggs performances were decidedly low key.

But despite his lacklustre efforts in the Tests, Briggs did manage to carve out another piece of cricketing history for himself when he appeared in the famous Smokers versus Non-Smokers match with the sides drawn from the Australian and England teams, at the little known East Melbourne ground in Victoria, which only ever hosted four first-class matches and was used mainly as a venue for Australian Rules football with its tenants being Essendon and University. The historic cricket match was a four-day eleven-a-side game which was admitted to the first-class records and Briggs' claim to fame was that he became the first bowler to take a wicket when the opposition had 800 on the board when he caught and bowled Maidstone-born William Cooper with the total on 803. Johnny was never one to give up the ghost! With Barnes absent hurt, the Non-Smokers closed on 803 for 9. Another record had also been set a few runs earlier when the Non-Smokers became the first to reach 800 in first-class cricket. Briggs, a pipe smoker, did well with the bat, scoring 86 and 54 in his two innings. With the ball, Briggs worked equally hard, sending down 55.1 of his side's 302 four-ball overs for a return of 4 for 144. The Smokers were forced to follow on, but held out for a draw with the Non-Smokers, rather surprisingly, running out of puff. With the score on 135 for 4, William Scotton blocked the last ball of the match and picked it up with the intention of keeping it as a souvenir, but the fielders appealed and Scotton was given out 'handled the ball'.

Briggs figures on two sets of cigarette cards produced by W.D. and H.O.Wills. The 1896 set, which features 50 players, is extremely rare and was retailing for £4,000 at the time of writing. A further set, also featuring 50 players, was issued in 1901 and sells for £1,000. There is, however, a reprint of the 1896 set, which retails for less than £50 framed. Unframed, the set can be bought for less than £10. Briggs was also featured twice on a set issued in 1901 by Ogden's in the 'Our Leading Cricketers' series which was given away with their popular Tab cigarettes, which the company proudly proclaimed were 'British made by British Labour'. In one card, Briggs is shown in a posed picture of his bowling action and in the other he is captured by the camera relaxing on a chair.

Three years earlier, the only other Smokers versus Non-Smokers game in history was held at Lord's, which resulted in a nine-wicket win for the Non-Smokers. Briggs did not play in this game, but two of his Lancashire team-mates, Barlow and Pilling, were in the Non-Smokers side.

In 1923, 36 years after the event, Lancashire CCC had been presented with the gold medal, given to Briggs by the Prince of Wales, later King Edward VII, to mark Briggs' achievement in making the highest individual score (33, in a low-scoring game) in the Test against Australia at Sydney in January 1887. The medal was in the shape of a shield with the royal coat of arms at the top. On an inner shield was an inscription and the initials JB, studded with seven diamonds. Between the initials was a miniature solid gold cricket bat. The medal was handed over to the club president, Oswald Lancashire, during the North v South match at Old Trafford in 1923. Seven years later, the *City News* revealed that the medal had been stolen.

Chapter Six
Taking a hundred wickets for the first time

'I always feels satisfied if I come out first or second in the bowling analysis and have an average of 20-odd runs at the end of the season; that ought to be a satisfactory result for anybody.' Johnny Briggs

Returning from Australia, Briggs settled down once more with Lancashire, playing in 17 matches in the 1887 season, scoring six fifties in a 736-run aggregate for an average of 27.25. He was the side's leading run scorer. But his bowling took on a new dimension. Briggs sent down 5,521 balls for Lancashire – only Watson (6,130 deliveries) was utilised more – and was rewarded with 102 wickets at 16.90 each with nine five-wicket hauls and one ten-wickets-in-a-match performance. Watson wasn't far behind him capturing exactly 100 wickets in the season.

Taking 100 wickets in a season for Lancashire for the first time marked Briggs out as a serious bowler – in all he took 114 wickets that year –and only Lohmann (154 wickets) was ahead of him in the national list. For once there was no major touring side visiting these shores with the best of the foreign opposition a team of Canadian amateurs. For this reason domestic representative games became all-important. The biggest of these was MCC versus

On 8 June 1887, Briggs achieved the astonishing feat of six wickets in six balls playing at Nantwich in Cheshire for A.N.Hornby's team against a team of 15 local cricketers from the neighbouring village of Minshull Vernon. The fixture marked the opening of a private cricket ground Hornby had laid out adjoining his home at Parkfield. Five of the wickets were taken before lunch and the sixth with the first ball after the interval. What is even more surprising is that all Briggs' victims were clean bowled. He finished with 11 for 5 although some reports suggest his figures were, in fact, 17 for 11, and at one period he claimed 11 wickets for no runs. To add to his extraordinary bowling performance, Briggs also scored a hard-hitting 90.

England at Lord's in early June, which marked MCC's centenary. Briggs played for the England XI, opening the bowling with Lohmann, and took seven wickets in the match which resulted in an innings victory for England. Briggs' wickets included W.G.Grace – caught and bowled – in MCC's second innings. He also played in both Gentlemen versus Players matches in London – at Lord's and The Oval – in mid-July.

Now established as England's best slow bowler – Lohmann was considered to be 'brisk medium' – Briggs was soon on his way back to Australia on one of Shaw and Shrewsbury's Antipodean sorties. So two months after Briggs had appeared in Lancashire's last match of the season against Yorkshire at Old Trafford, he was on the field again in Australia. This time, though, there was a problem – there were two separate tours of Australia. Bizarrely, they both set off on the same ship, the *Iberia* from Tilbury and Plymouth. The touring party which included Briggs was organised by Shrewsbury and Shaw together with the trustees of the Sydney Cricket Club. The other, usually referred to as G.F.Vernon's XI, was organised through the Melbourne Cricket Ground – a fairly early example of cricket shooting itself in the foot or rather both feet.

The two sides had the normal complement of 13 players, with a mix of professionals and amateurs, but it was Vernon's party which seems to have been thought of as more respectable than Shaw and Shrewsbury's side, even though the latter was captained by Aubrey Smith. The fact that two sides set sail for Australia underlines the absence of a central cricket authority in either England or Australia. The latter had some excuse – she consisted of six colonies plus various territories, each governed separately. Afterwards *Wisden* commented that the twin tours were 'a piece of folly that will not be perpetrated again'. Shaw and Shrewsbury

---

Briggs bowled 831 maiden four-ball overs in 1887, the most he bowled in a season. Even when overs had six balls, he got through his overs incredibly quickly. Off his short run, which usually consisted of just two paces, Briggs had been timed at 'just over 44 seconds' in a match at Old Trafford, according to a newspaper cutting from 1900. In the over timed, five of the balls went straight back to the bowler and the other went to Arthur Mold at mid-on. Another spectator – 'a clerical gentleman' – had timed a Briggs' over at 47.5 seconds. Muttiah Muralitharan can bowl a maiden in less than two minutes, but not by much.

would have nodded in agreement with that comment as they suffered a loss of £2,400 on this tour. On the field, though, both touring sides were successful although they were brought together on only one occasion – a game against a Combined Australian XI, which has been treated as a Test match since 1890. Briggs was one of the 11 players chosen from the 26 who would have been available for this match. This one-off Test, held at the Sydney Cricket Ground, started on 10 February, 1888. Briggs did little to justify his selection, making 0 and 14 and he wasn't called upon to bowl as Lohmann and Peel ripped through the Aussies twice, with England completing a comprehensive win on the fifth day of this timeless Test. They had, in fact, only needed three days to polish off Australia as no play was possible on days two and three.

On this 1887/88 tour, Shaw and Shrewsbury's side played 26 matches in all, 19 of them against odds sides. If anything, the travelling by sea, rail and horse-drawn coach was more taxing than the tour of 1884/85, with matches in Australia as far apart as Adelaide in South Australia, Maryborough in Queensland and Bourke in northern New South Wales, which is almost 400 miles from Sydney. In fact, the Australians have a saying 'back of Bourke' which is similar to the oft-used 'back of beyond' and gives some indication of the distances travelled.

After Australia, the tourists went on to New Zealand, crossing the Tasman Sea in very heavy weather, playing three matches – in Wellington, on North Island, and at Christchurch on South Island – on their eventual arrival. In New Zealand, Briggs had figures of 8 for 41 versus Wellington Twenty Two at Wellington and 9 for 43 versus Canterbury Eighteen at Christchurch and 9 for 26 against the same side in a second match at the same venue.

They set off on their return journey to England from Port Lyttelton on the *SS Coptic* on March 31. Summing up the tour, *Wisden* reported that 'Lohmann, Briggs and Shrewsbury were the mainstays of the side'. In the odds matches, Briggs scored 481 runs and took 178 wickets at an average cost of 5.16. In eight first-class matches in Australia, including the 'Combined' match, he scored 229 runs at 19.08 and took 30 wickets at 14.46. His highest first-class score was 75 against Victoria at the MCG just before Christmas and his best bowling was 6 for 40 against 'An Australian XI' at Sydney where he and Lohmann, bowling unchanged through both innings, bundled out the opposition twice inside two days. Briggs played in many odds matches and produced some remarkable analyses on the tour, including match figures of 16 for 66 v Queensland Eighteen at Brisbane. At the end of the tour Briggs was owed £60 by Shaw and Shrewsbury, whose finances were by now in some disarray. Briggs had to wait for his money as did some of the amateurs who were due even larger sums.

Briggs arrived back in England just in time for the 1888 domestic season, in which he scored, in all his first-class matches, 872 runs at 21.26, including one century and four 50s and took 160 wickets at 10.49 with 16 five-wicket hauls, four times claiming ten in a match. Although his county had a poor season against other counties, he was instrumental in helping Lancashire defeat a strong Australian side at Old Trafford, returning figures of 4 for 34 and 5 for 15.

Briggs' all-round displays saw him finish third among his fellow professionals in the national batting averages and second in the bowling averages. With 648 runs, he was the county's leading scorer for the second time in his career. The *City News* reporter, employing the sort of hyperbole which is prevalent in the sports pages of some of today's tabloids, said of his bowling skills: 'The way in which he breaks his first ball from an impossible distance from the off, his second ball from an equally impossible distance from the leg, and then comes a perfectly straight one, as fast as Spofforth's fastest, must be watched to be believed. No wonder batters give him up in despair.'

His performances earned him the accolade of one of the first set of *Wisden*'s cricketers of the year. Briggs was chosen along with Lohmann and Peel and the Australian trio of John Ferris, Charlie Turner and Sammy Woods, all of them bowlers. The following year, *Wisden* continued the theme choosing no fewer than nine batsmen. In his preface to the 1889 *Wisden*, the editor, Charles Pardon, wrote that to mark the extraordinary success of the sextet, the Almanack was including their six portraits specially taken by the leading cricket photographers, Messrs Hawkins of Brighton. *Wisden*'s notes on Briggs said 'he has been justly regarded as one of the most able and destructive bowlers in the country'. Between them in eleven-a-side cricket in 1888 (not all first-class), they took 1,272 wickets at an average cost of 11.89. Turner alone had 314 victims. In first-class cricket the six of them had between them snared 1,109 wickets at a combined average of 12.43. Clearly, they were the six leading bowlers in the world at that time.

Lancashire line-up 1888:
Briggs (cross-legged on the ground, right, front row) with Alex Watson.
Back row: George Baker, Frank Sugg, Frank Taylor, Dick Barlow, Ernest Steel,
George Yates.
Middle row: Sidney Crosfield, Albert Hornby, Dick Pilling, Joseph Eccles.

Ferris, a deadly left-arm swing bowler, had the distinction of playing Tests for both Australia and England. He and Turner, bowling unchanged, wreaked havoc on England in the First Test at Sydney in January 1887 where England were all out for 45. Remarkably, England were to turn things around to such an extent that they eventually won a dramatic match by 13 runs. Briggs, in fact, top scored with 33 in England's second innings. Ferris, who was later to become one of Briggs' hat-trick victims when he performed the feat for the North versus the South at Scarborough in 1891, was only 33 when he died of enteric fever in Durban in 1900, during the Boer War, where he was serving with the British army. Woods also played for Australia and England and served Somerset well for 12 seasons, later becoming club secretary.

After his exertions on the tour of Australia and New Zealand, Briggs, for the first time in several years, was able to put his feet up, probably relaxing by playing his beloved billiards at his local pub. He had played his last game of cricket on 18 September, 1888 and it wasn't until 21 November that he was to set sail for his one and only tour of South Africa. The tour was organised by Major R.G.Warton, a member of the Army General Staff in Cape Town. He was prominent in local cricket circles and was a member of Western Province CC. He came to England to make arrangements for the tour and as a result the side was known as Major Warton's team. Warton was educated at Highgate School in north London and is listed as a famous Old Cholmeleian, a distinction he shares with Philip Tufnell, the former Middlesex and England off-spinner, who also attended Highgate. In addition to managing the team, Warton stood as an umpire in both Tests in the series. The side was captained by Charles Aubrey Smith, who had captained Sussex in 1888 and had been on Shaw and Shrewsbury's tour to Australia and New Zealand the previous winter.

The tourists set out from England on the *Garth Castle* on 21 November, calling at Lisbon and Madeira en route and arrived at Cape Town on 14 December. Like the *Orient*, on which Briggs had first sailed to Australia, the *Garth Castle* was built by John Elder and Company on the Clyde. She was named after Sir Donald Currie's estate in Scotland. The link with Currie continued when at a farewell banquet on board, Currie, who was head of the Castle Mail Packets Company, presented a cup to be awarded by the English team to the side which had excelled most against them. On handing over the trophy, Currie said: 'I think the cricketers out there would like to keep the cup among themselves in recollection of your visit and as a gift from myself.' Kimberley had the distinction of winning the inaugural trophy and the Currie Cup was for many years the equivalent of England's county championship. The rugby union version of the Currie Cup was established four years later and is still South Africa's premier regional tournament. The tour was less physically demanding than previous Australasian tours with matches played over a 50-day period between 21 December, 1888 and 26 March, 1889. They travelled around 3,000 miles utilising a variety of modes of transport, including bullock carts in places, to fulfil a fixture list which comprised of 19 matches, 17 against odds sides. Most of the games were on matting or compacted soil pitches.

It was on this tour that Briggs produced one of the most sensational bowling performances in Test match history. It happened in the Second Test of the two-match series, which England won 2-0, although the games were not afforded Test match status until 1907. In fact, the England touring party was a mixed bunch containing acknowledged stars like Briggs, Surrey's Bobby Abel and Ulyett, who had replaced James Roberts who was forced to return home after a family bereavement, while some of the other tourists were reckoned only to be of good club standard.

Briggs made his initial Test appearance on South African soil in the first match of the series, played on a matting wicket, at the Crusaders' Ground, St George's Park, Port Elizabeth, starting on 12 March, 1889. Scheduled for three days, the match was over just before 3.30pm on the second day. Briggs helped his England team-mates to a comprehensive eight-wicket win, taking 4 for 39 and 4 for 19 although he was a let-down with the bat, failing to trouble the scorers. He again did next to nothing with the bat in the Second and final Test at Cape Town later that month, going in at No.3 and scoring only six. But he was absolutely devastating with the ball, taking 7 for 17 in South Africa's first innings total of 47 and 8 for 11 as the hosts crashed to 43 in their second innings, sealing an innings and 202-run win for England. Once more, it was all over after two days of a scheduled three-day game.

On the first day, England totalled 292 all out, with Abel (120) scoring the first first-class hundred in South Africa. By the close South Africa were already struggling at 2 for 1. But worse – much worse – was to follow on day two for the home side. Briggs was virtually unplayable, taking seven of the remaining nine wickets for 17 runs in 18.1 overs. Following on, South Africa were in dire straits once again. By lunch, they were rocking at 36 for 7, Briggs having taken five wickets for nine runs in 13 overs. Briggs wrapped up the South Africa innings – and an England victory – by taking the remaining three wickets just after lunch. During the morning session, Briggs had taken 12 wickets for 26 runs in 31.1 overs – a measure of his accuracy can be gauged by the fact that eleven of his victims were bowled with the other lbw. It is almost certainly the most destructive pre-lunch Test spell of all time.

England's victorious captain was Surrey's Monty Bowden, the youngest ever at 23 years 144 days. He was leading the side for the first time in this Test, having taken over from Aubrey Smith, who had skippered the side in the first match of the series. Tragically, Bowden died at an even earlier age than Briggs. He enjoyed the South African way of life so much that he and Aubrey Smith stayed on after the tour to set up a stock broking partnership. He even represented Transvaal in domestic first-class cricket. But after travelling north to Rhodesia he died in Umtali (now Mutare) Hospital in Mashonaland in February 1892 where it is said that his body had to be protected from marauding lions prior to its interment in a coffin made from whisky cases. He was only 26. Like Briggs, it was officially recorded that Bowden's death was due to an attack of epilepsy. However, a fall from his cart, leading to Bowden being trampled underfoot by his own oxen, may well have contributed to the young man's demise.

Life was much sweeter for Bowden's fellow-captain Aubrey Smith, who played in just the one Test as well as for Cambridge University and Sussex. He survived reading about his own death from pneumonia in the *Graaff-Reinet Advertiser* to become a Hollywood actor, starring alongside such screen legends as Elizabeth Taylor, Clark Gable, Laurence Olivier, Vivien Leigh, Ronald Colman and Gary Cooper. Standing more than 6ft tall and with his fine moustache, Aubrey Smith, who later became Sir Charles Aubrey Smith, was one of the most instantly recognisable faces in the movies. He played a series of colonels, generals and majors with great aplomb. He was knighted in 1944 and died at the ripe old age of 85 – ironically from pneumonia – in Beverly Hills, California in 1948, where he had helped set up the Hollywood cricket club.

Although Briggs' tour will most be remembered for his devastating performance in the Second Test, he also had astonishing success in the odds matches. At Port Elizabeth, against an Eastern District XXII, his first innings haul was 16 for 94 and he returned a scarcely believable 27 for 23 (15 for 4 and 12 for 19) against Twenty Two of Cape Mounted Rifles at King William's Town. Once again, he proved a willing workhorse for his captain and in the 37 innings in which he bowled he continued at one end, unchanged, in 21 of

Briggs possessed amazing reserves of stamina. For Lancashire he bowled unchanged throughout a match with Barlow v Gloucestershire at Liverpool in 1888; five times with Mold v Sussex at Hove, 1891; v Kent at the Angel Ground, Tonbridge, 1892; v Nottinghamshire at Trent Bridge, 1895; v Middlesex at Lord's, 1895 and v Leicestershire at Grace Road, Leicester, 1895. In the latter two matches, Briggs and Mold displayed remarkable durability as the games were played in the same week, Briggs sending down 94.3 five-ball overs and Mold bowling 95 overs. Briggs also bowled unchanged in tandem with Alec Watson v Sussex at Old Trafford, 1890, in several matches with minor counties and against Scotland at Edinburgh in 1895. He also bowled unchanged with Lohmann for Shrewsbury's XI against Australia at Sydney in 1887/88.

them. *Wisden* said Briggs was 'literally doing marvels' with the ball, adding the rider 'the generous hospitality had a bad effect on the cricket' with no further explanation. None was needed. Under the influence or not, Briggs was taking wickets for fun, with a scarcely believable total of 269 victims for 1,411 runs. With the bat, his highest score was 93 not out against Kimberley XVIII at Kimberley.

Chapter Seven
Sharing the Championship

'In 1889 on the County Ground, Bristol, I remember he was quite unplayable and I preferred to keep at the end Mold bowled at, and was not out 37 out of 87.' W.G.Grace

The following campaign, 1889, Briggs once again led the way among the Lancashire bowlers with 103 wickets at 11.84, helping Lancashire to a share of the championship with Surrey and their old protagonists Nottinghamshire. He had 11 five-wicket hauls and three 10-wicket matches. But by now Briggs' workload had been lessened considerably by the emergence of the Northamptonshire-born fast bowler Arthur Mold, who in his first first-class season at Old Trafford, took 92 wickets at an average of 12.32, not all that far behind Briggs' own contribution.

Briggs sent down 3,756 deliveries for the county in 1889, but in the previous two seasons his totals were 4,167 (1888) and 5,521 (1887). With the bat, Briggs scored 439 runs for the county at an average of 20.90 with two half-centuries. Lancashire had the

Briggs' bowling partner Mold was a highly contentious figure in an era when suspect bowling actions were becoming an increasing problem. *Wisden* had thought that he should 'take care' with his bowling action as early as 1888. There was no doubting his speed and his movement off the pitch – he was, in fact, a perfect foil for Briggs – but his action came under closer and closer scrutiny and he was restricted to only three Test appearances. In 1900 he was no balled by Australian-born umpire Jim Phillips and a meeting of county captains at the end of that season voted 11-1 that his action was illegal. In the following season, he was no-balled 16 times in ten overs in Lancashire's match against Somerset at Manchester, again by Phillips and although no other umpire called Mold, he drifted out of first-class cricket, ending his playing days in the Northamptonshire leagues. He spent his retirement shooting, running a pub and looking after his mother.

satisfaction of beating their fellow-champions Surrey twice – both times by convincing margins – but they lost heavily to Nottinghamshire at Trent Bridge although in the return match at Old Trafford, they had Nottinghamshire in trouble at 69 for 8, with Briggs taking 4 for 32, in the only innings possible after rain had ruled out play on the first and third days so Lancashire's hopes of clinching an outright title were washed away. They had won ten of their 14 games against other counties.

In addition to Mold, two other players joined the Lancashire roster, Belfast-born batsman Albert Paul, whose association with the county was to stretch into the 1930s, and Yorkshireman Albert Ward, who topped the county batting averages with 33.65. Paul and Ward took the route Briggs had when he made his county debut, playing in a colts match. The pair were appearing for the Colts of the North against the Colts of South at Lord's at the beginning of May and, as Lancashire were playing MCC in St John's Wood later that week, they were asked stay on in London prior to their first-team debuts. They made auspicious starts, Paul top-scoring with 36 in the first innings and Ward making an unbeaten 62 out of 134 in the second innings.

Pugnacious:
Briggs in determined mood in this
posed photograph

Later in the season, Briggs made a telling contribution to a remarkable Roses match at Huddersfield, although it was with the bat rather than the ball. In a low-scoring contest, Briggs top-scored with 25 and 41 as Lancashire mustered only 81 all out in the first innings and 153 in their second knock. Yorkshire fared marginally worse, scoring 160 and 71 as they went down to a dramatic three-run defeat.

The 1890 domestic season was another good one for Briggs, who played in 26 matches in total, scoring 708 runs (at 18.63), and taking 158 wickets (at 12.34), which did put him top among the regular bowlers. Against Sussex at Manchester,

Briggs turned in a remarkable performance with both bat and ball. He scored 129 not out as Lancashire declared on 246 for 2 after the first day's play had been washed out. His unbeaten partnership of 215 with Ward for the third wicket was the highest he was ever involved with in first-class cricket. Briggs then took five wickets in seven balls at no cost as he and Watson skittled out their opponents for 35 and 24 to record an innings victory. Briggs' figures were 5 for 25 and 5 for 16 with Watson taking 5 for 7 and 4 for 6. The Sussex first innings total was the lowest ever innings total at Old Trafford and their combined innings total of 59 is the second lowest aggregate in a championship match. It was arguably Briggs finest all-round performance for Lancashire.

On the international front, Briggs missed the first two Tests against Australia – at Lord's and The Oval – because of injury and was brought back for the Third and final Test at Old Trafford in August, although frustratingly, the match was abandoned without a ball being bowled. He did, however, play twice against the Australians for the North of England, at Old Trafford, in June and at Headingley in September. His most notable performance against the tourists was at Scarborough for Lord Londesborough's XI in September. It was on the North Marine Road ground that Briggs set bowling figures that stand to this day as the best ever at the venue. Briggs took 15-57 (9 for 31 and 6 for 26). He might have captured all ten in the first innings but for the fact that the Australians' No.7, Percie Charlton, was run out. In a low-scoring match, the visitors were bowled out for 77 and 60 with Lord Londesborough's XI, captained by W.G.Grace, making 39 and 90 as the Australians recorded an eight-run victory.

Domestically, the season was probably most memorable from Lancashire's point of view for the debut of an 18-year-old, only a few weeks out of Harrow School, one A.C. 'Archie' MacLaren. He was destined to become one of the greats of the game and was to captain both the Old Trafford club and his country in a long, distinguished and often controversial career. MacLaren played in 35 Tests, scoring 1,931 runs at an average of 33.87, and in all first-class cricket totalled more than 22,000 runs at an average of 34.15. He scored five Test centuries and a further 42 in other first-class matches. He will be remembered for his mammoth effort for Lancashire against Somerset at Taunton in 1895 when he was finally dismissed for 424, an individual score which has never been bettered in the club's history. Although his quadruple century was a tour de force, perhaps MacLaren's greatest achievement was in 1921, when he boasted that he could pick a team to beat Warwick Armstrong's all-conquering Australians. MacLaren selected 11 amateurs and despite being bowled out for 43 in their first knock and conceding a first innings lead of 130 in the match played in Eastbourne at late August, MacLaren's team gained an unlikely triumph by 28 runs.

The following domestic season, 1891, another MacLaren made his first appearance in Lancashire's ranks with the debut of Archie's older brother James. His was to be an undistinguished career for the Red Rose, playing just four matches between 1891 and 1894, scoring nine runs for an average of 2.25 and a highest score of six. He didn't bowl. Unlike his younger sibling who eschewed a university education in order to earn a living at cricket, James chose to become a doctor and played cricket at club level for Bowden CC. Briggs' 1891 season was very much as you were as far as his bowling was concerned – 128 wickets at 13.22 in all matches, but his batting had dropped away quite markedly and his batting average wasn't dissimilar to his bowling average (371 runs at 12.38).

Chapter Eight
A Test hat-trick

'Briggs got most of his wickets with his leg breaks, especially when the ground was soft; but on good fast wickets I found the ball that gave me most trouble was the one he pitched on or just outside off stump and came in with his arm.' W.G.Grace

It is not clear how 'hat-trick' came into the cricketing vocabulary, but it is believed it was first used after a match at Sheffield's Hyde Park ground in 1858 when an All-England team took on a Hallam XI.

During the game, Heathfield Stephenson, of the All-England XI, took three wickets in successive balls. As was customary at the time for rewarding outstanding sporting feats, a collection was made and the proceeds were used to buy a hat, which was duly presented to Stephenson. Thus the hat-trick was born. Esher-born Stephenson was a Surrey stalwart between 1853 and 1871, scoring more than 7,000 runs and taking in excess of 300 wickets. After his retirement, he umpired in one Test – against Australia on his home ground at the age of 47, nine years after his last match for Surrey and 32 years after his hat-trick achievement.

Whatever the origin of the term hat-trick, they are rare birds in Test cricket. At the time of writing, the feat had been achieved on 36 occasions since the first Test match in 1877. The first bowler to have his name inscribed on the Test match hat-trick roll of honour was Australia's Fred 'The Demon' Spofforth who took three-in-three against England at Melbourne on 2 January, 1879, while the most recent was Indian fast bowler Irfan Pathan on 29 January, 2006 against Pakistan in Karachi in the 1,783rd Test match on record. Spofforth had a remarkable match, his hat-trick apart,

Briggs, in addition to his famous hat-trick at Sydney in 1892, achieved 'three-in-three' for North v South at Scarborough in the previous year. Briggs' victims were Billy Murdoch, Edward Hadow and J.J.Ferris.

claiming 6 for 48 in the first innings and 7 for 62 in the second as the Aussies won by 10 wickets.

Spofforth was an uncompromising character and refused to play in Australia's first ever Test match because his New South Wales colleague, wicket-keeper Billy Murdoch, had been overlooked by the selectors. It was only when Murdoch was picked for the second Test that Spofforth agreed to make his international debut. In 1996, Spofforth was inducted into the Australian Cricket Hall of Fame when the original ten members were chosen.

Left-arm pace bowler Pathan exploded on to the Indian Test scene at the age of 19 and at one time was considered a successor to the great Kapil Dev, but not long after his hat-trick – the first achieved in the first over of a Test – his bowling form nosedived despite an improvement in his prowess with the bat and he became the first Indian player to be sent home from a tour (South Africa) to concentrate on domestic cricket. Pathan dismissed Salman Butt (caught low down at first slip), Younis Khan (lbw) and Mohammad Yousuf (clean bowled) with the fourth, fifth and sixth deliveries of the match, and at close of play he told the media: 'There was some moisture in the wicket this morning. It was doing a lot off the seam but there was not much movement in the air.'

Asked what was going through his mind ahead of his third ball, Pathan added: 'I've been on a hat-trick twice in international cricket and I told myself that if it didn't happen before, it may not happen today. I just told myself to try to bowl stump to stump. I didn't realise it would actually happen. It's a dream for anyone and it's wonderful for me to get a hat-trick in the first over.' In those considerably less media-friendly days of the latter stages of the nineteenth century, it isn't recorded what Briggs' thought process was as he skipped in off his two-pace run in a bid to complete his hat-trick. Nevertheless, his achievement must have given him immense satisfaction even though it failed to turn the match England's way. In his hat-trick match, Briggs had made little impression with the ball in the first innings of the Australia-England Test, which began at the Sydney Cricket Ground on 29 January, 1892, taking 0 for 24 in his ten overs. Lohmann was the star of the show with figures of 8 for 58 as the hosts were dismissed for only 144 after Australia's wicket-keeper captain Jack Blackham had won the toss and elected to take first knock. England were 38 for 0 at the close with W.G.Grace and Abel making a confident start and the visitors continued in much the same vein on the second day, going past the Australian total with only four wickets down. Briggs appeared on the scene with the England score 178 for 7 – a lead of 34 – and he and Abel attacked freely in a stand of 57 to which Briggs contributed a valuable 28 before he was adjudged lbw to a Harry Trott leg break. With help from the tail, and especially from No.11 John Sharpe, who had only one eye and who played in only three Tests, Abel managed to complete a magnificent unbeaten 132 and in so doing became the first Englishman to carry his bat in a Test innings. England, all out for 307, had a more than healthy lead of 163 runs.

By the close of day two the Australians were in further trouble at 1 for 1 with Trott, promoted from No.7 to open the innings, caught by Sharpe at mid-on off the bowling of Lohmann. However, by the end of day three the Australians were fighting back magnificently and closed on 263 for 3 with John Lyons having compiled a marvellous 134 and the obdurate Alec Bannerman on 67 not out, having batted the whole day. On a rain-interrupted fourth day, the Australians continued to pile on the runs with Bannerman proving difficult to dislodge. Briggs was introduced into the attack and finally got rid of Bannerman, caught at point by Grace, for 91, an innings which had occupied 448 minutes and contained only three boundaries.

By now Charlie Turner had joined Bob McLeod at the crease and the pair struggled against the bowling of Peel and Briggs. It was at this point that Briggs wrote his name into Test history, becoming the first man to add to an Ashes century with a hat-trick although the *Wisden* Almanack of the following year completely failed to mention his momentous achievement in its match report!

Briggs struck first when he had Turner bowled; next ball he won an lbw decision against the Australian captain Blackham and then he applied the coup de grace with the wicket of Sydney Callaway – named after the city of his birth – caught at point by Grace. Australia had been bowled out for 391, but unfortunately Briggs' work was undone when England could muster only 156, leaving Australia with a 72-run margin of victory.

With the series already won by Australia, England were easy winners of the third and final Test at the Adelaide Oval, amassing an unassailable 499 all out in the first innings with Stoddart scoring 134 and Briggs making 39. This time Briggs' work with the ball wasn't wasted as he took 6 for 49 and 6 for 87 as England triumphed by an innings and 230 runs, Australia succumbing for 100 and 169 in their two innings. It cut the home side's series-winning margin to 2-1.

Thus the tour ended in defeat. It had been financed by Lord Sheffield under Shaw's management and was considered more 'establishment' than 'commercial'. All the top players of the day apart from Shrewsbury and Gunn took part. The side was captained by W.G.Grace, who commanded a huge fee in spite of his amateur status. Briggs had been included in the 13, despite the presence of another slow left-armer Peel, although he was often played as a middle-order batsman and was in the side as an all-rounder, with Briggs employed as a specialist bowler. Although the side played eight eleven-a-side matches, which were afforded first-class status, they were also obliged to fulfil 19 games against odds sides, travelling across tracts of South Australia, Victoria and New South Wales, and venturing, for the first time, to Tasmania. Grace shared out the bowling more equitably than on some previous tours in these odds matches, but Briggs still managed to take 108 wickets at 6.04. However, against Twenty Four of Bowral, the home town many years later of the legendary Donald Bradman, Briggs bowled almost unchanged through two innings for a 24-wicket haul. As usual on these occasions, it was left to *Wisden* to put things into perspective, describing the home cricketers as a 'poor lot'.

Chapter Nine
Match double against Yorkshire

'Merry Johnny' was then and for many years afterwards one of the most formidable of Australia's opponents, and had he been a more reliable batsman he would, to my mind, have ranked with A.G.Steel as an all-round player next to W.G.' George Giffen

There was no rest for Briggs and the 1892 domestic season began on the first Monday after Lord Sheffield's side returned to England following a six-week sea voyage. The Lancashire man was back 'at the office' opening the bowling, alongside Watson, against MCC at Lord's. In MCC's first innings he bowled 63 five-ball overs and conceded only 86 runs. Later that week he played for C.I.Thornton's XI at Cambridge, and the following week, he was in Lord Sheffield's side in a special benefit match for their manager Alfred Shaw, at Trent Bridge in cold, showery weather.

There can be little doubt that Briggs' services were still much in demand, but he played in few of the big representative games during the season, missing all three Gentlemen versus Players fixtures and the end-of-season festival matches. He did, however, turn out for the Married versus Single at Lord's in a well-attended benefit match for the former Yorkshire, Northumberland and Lincolnshire fast bowler Robert Clayton over the Whitsun Bank Holiday and for North versus South at Edgbaston in late June.

This was a largely domestic season without any major touring attractions and the county championship was of most interest to cricket followers. Lancashire made a poor start to their county matches, losing two of their first six games and were thus – the points system made deductions for losses – scarcely in contention for the title. Lancashire's bowling was almost entirely entrusted to Briggs, Mold and Watson. Once again Briggs topped 100 wickets with 124 victims in all first-class matches at 13.75 and his run-scoring improved with 569 at 16.73. In the championship he took 85 wickets at 13.62. Roses matches against the 'auld enemy' Yorkshire always brought out the best in a man as competitive as

Briggs – he took 170 White Rose wickets at less than 16 runs each in matches between the neighbouring counties – and it was in the August Bank Holiday game against the Tykes at Manchester that Briggs performed the 'match double' of 100 runs and ten wickets. He had achieved the feat against Sussex at Old Trafford in 1890 and later against Surrey at The Oval. He came mighty close in the match against Sussex at Old Trafford in 1888, scoring one and 126 not out and taking 9-88 in the only innings in which he bowled. In the Roses match, Briggs scored 115 and had match figures of 13-209.

With no tourists to play during the summer, the sequence continued into the winter of 1892/93 and Briggs remained in England with the only tour leaving these shores an all-amateur side under the stewardship of Lord Hawke which went off to play in India and Ceylon.

The following season – 1893 – another Roses match provided another highlight in Briggs' career. It happened at Old Trafford in August 1893. It was the lowest-scoring games in the history of the series and still retains the record for the lowest aggregate number of runs in a completed championship match in which all 40 wickets fell.

Sydney Crossfield won the toss and decided to bat. Even by normal circumspect Roses standards it was slow going and Lancashire were always struggling against the accuracy of the Yorkshire attack. They managed to scramble together a total of 64 in 59.3 five-ball overs, a scoring rate of just over one an over. Roses debutant George Hirst, Peel and Ernest Smith shared the wickets between them with only three Lancashire batsmen getting into double figures. Briggs scored nought.

Despite such a meagre total, Briggs bowled Lancashire to a first innings lead, his 22 five-ball overs bringing him 6 for 35. Mold grabbed the other four wickets, the pair bowling unchanged as Yorks succumbed for 58, a deficit of six runs. Lancashire fared even worse in their second innings, managing only 50 with Peel (6 for 24) and Ted Wainwright, who hadn't been called upon to bowl in the first innings, mopping up the rest of the wickets in a remarkable return of 4 for 8.

It left Yorkshire with the tricky task of scoring 57 to win in a match where scores had steadily been in decline since the first day. But they made a marvellous start with openers Arthur Sellers and

Stanley Jackson taking the score along to 24 for 0, close to half the total needed, before the first wicket went down. Sellers fell to the left-arm medium pace of William Oakley, while Jackson was run out.

Thereafter it was very much a case of Yorkshire versus Briggs. But Briggs couldn't bowl at both ends and Crosfield eventually took him out of the attack. However, with Yorkshire needing just six to win and their last pair at the crease, Crosfield brought Briggs back, although the *Manchester Guardian* of the day reported that it was Hornby who made the decision – Hornby, in fact, was missing from the Lancashire line-up. Perhaps the *Guardian's* correspondent was overcome by the sheer excitement of the occasion. Crosfield had taken a calculated risk. Briggs placed his field carefully, waving Albert Ward to the boundary. Briggs was bowling to Yorkshire No.8 George Ulyett, a popular cricketer who had earned the nickname 'Happy Jack'. The Tykes' skipper, who played in goal for Sheffield Wednesday and on his retirement from sport became a publican in Sheffield after a short spell as a first-class umpire, favoured an attacking approach.

Briggs knew that if he tossed one up, Ulyett would take the bait. Briggs also knew the risks in such a policy. Nevertheless he tempted Ulyett, shaping to bowl a slow delivery but finding an extra three or four yards of pace. The extra speed was enough to confuse Ulyett and although he appeared to get hold of it, he only succeeded in lofting it into the waiting hands of the reliable Ward, fielding on the fence. It was Briggs' eleventh wicket of a remarkable match and, to the delight of the majority of the big crowd, Lancashire had sealed victory by six runs. The home crowd was happy enough, but it is said that afterwards Briggs sat ashen-faced in the dressing room, as the enormity of the gamble he had taken sank in.

Despite this famous win, Lancashire had to settle for second place behind Yorkshire in the race for the title. At one stage they racked up six straight wins, but lost the final two matches, which cost them the championship. Yorkshire had set a furious pace, winning their first five games and from then on Lancashire were forced to play catch-up. With Watson dropping out of the side, Briggs and Mold were worked very hard indeed. Between them they bowled 1,662 of the 2,200 overs sent down by the county, and took 225 of the county's 282 wickets in the competition; a remarkable 80 per cent of wickets to fall. In all games they matched each other wicket for wicket, taking 166 each, with Briggs' victims costing him 15.89 apiece and Mold averaging 16.96.

It was during this season that Briggs dismissed Arthur Shrewsbury in the game against Nottinghamshire at Manchester with a first innings delivery that was perhaps a forerunner of Shane Warne's 'ball of the century' to dismiss England's Mike Gatting on the same Old Trafford ground in the 1993 Test against Australia. Shrewsbury, who for a decade starting in the late 1880s was considered the finest professional batsman in England, was adept at playing the ball with his pads and his dismissal is described in great detail by the *City News*: 'Shrewsbury, amongst other things, is the inventor of a style of playing the ball with his legs. Whenever a ball puzzles him or he, for any reason, feels uncomfortable about it, if it is not pitched straight he simply puts his leg before it and so keeps it out of the wickets.' 'The style is, if played with discretion, wonderfully effective from the point of view of sticking in. It breaks the bowler's heart, it worries the umpire well nigh to death, and it will eventually cause a change in the rule of leg before wicket, as it most assuredly ought to do.' 'But in this case, Briggs, who was bowling with his head as well as with his hand and arm, completely beat the great leg blocker at his own game to the unbounded joy of everybody round the field. Shrewsbury, bothered by a peculiar ball which was gyrating and twisting about in mid-air in a way which was eminently puzzling and which was apparently likely, if unstopped to take the off stump, quietly put his right leg in such a position that the ball could not possibly reach that point.' 'But in doing this he left the leg stump unguarded and the ball, as if actually inspired by Briggs' cunning, shot in between the batter's legs and hit the leg wicket.' 'The incident was one which will serve for many a bit of cricket gossip in years to come, and was worth in itself, to your true enthusiast, a year's waiting to see.'

The 1893 season was when the Australians toured this country, playing against three England sides, all of which were selected by the local ground authorities. Briggs was left out of the First Test at Lord's, with MCC apparently deciding they needed only one all-rounder. They went for Peel, six years older than Briggs, perhaps because he was a more solid batsman. But the major factor must have been that he had already proved a thorn in the Australians' side, taking 26 wickets against them in matches under various titles. It was the first time that Briggs had actually been 'dropped' from a Test side since he first played for his country in 1884/85. His only previous absences were when he was unavailable through injury in 1890 and in 1891/92 when he didn't play in South Africa because it clashed with a tour to Australia.

But even without any competition from his fellow left-armer, Peel couldn't continue the successful sequence at Lord's, scoring only 12 runs and failing to take a single wicket. The upshot was that at The Oval he was replaced by Briggs, who seized his chance with both hands, taking five wickets in each innings as England romped to an innings victory. Briggs' selection for the final Test – on his home ground – was a 'given'. However, the issue of competition with Peel for the all-rounder's slot did not arise as Yorkshire withheld the services of Peel, Jackson and Wainwright as they were still in contention for the county championship. Yorkshire were in clear breach of an agreement made by the counties in December 1892 that the counties would not keep players back in this way. Briggs again bowled well at Manchester, taking six wickets in a drawn match.

In August 1893, Briggs was playing at Stourbridge for Lancashire Second XI against Worcestershire Second XI, then a second-class county, when he received a telegram telling him that his wife,

Double joy:
Briggs with his beloved twins, John Hector and George

Alice, had given birth to twin boys. Remarkably, during the course of this two-day fixture, Edwards, the Worcestershire wicket-keeper, also received a telegram informing him that his wife had given birth to twin boys. Briggs, who had opened the Lancashire bowling with Mold, celebrated his good news with 4 for 44 and 3 for 26 as Lancashire swept to victory by an innings and 121 runs with Worcestershire bowled out for 80 and 49. It was a bit of an unequal struggle – Briggs was already an established Test cricketer, while just two days after the Stourbridge match ended on August 12, Mold, who took eight Worcestershire wickets, was in action, along with Briggs, for England against Australia at The Oval. Edwards, batting at No.10 for the home side, scored only 4 and 9.

After Briggs' twins were born a toy entitled 'Briggs's Twins' appeared on the market. The toy sold well but there is no record of the Briggs family receiving any royalties from its sale.

Chapter Ten
Mixed benefit

'I don't want to speak to you now my Lord.'   Johnny Briggs

Briggs was awarded a benefit by his club in 1894, when he was still only 31. It was a deserved recognition of his talents, work ethic and loyalty. He had by then given stalwart service to the county for 15 seasons and was one of the game's senior professionals. In fact, when in 1894, *Wisden* sought the views of players about the 'follow-on' controversy that was then taxing cricket's administrators, Briggs was one of the three professional players to whom they turned. The benefit match was, until after the Second World War, the principal source of income for a player in his benefit season. Since then, of course, benefits go on for many months and include golf days, dinners and auctions usually organised by a benefit committee and often involving sponsored events. There are also regular collections around the players' home ground during matches.

Briggs didn't have much luck with the weather – and Lord Hawke's reaction to it – during his benefit match against Yorkshire as we shall see. But the extent of the damage to Briggs' finances has been exaggerated, with perhaps the most extreme example being the comments by Mike Marqusee in his much praised book 'Anyone but England', first published in 1994, which asserts, even in its corrected second edition in 1998, that 'Johnny Briggs, a popular Lancashire and England slow bowler, requested a benefit after his fourteenth year with the county and was told it was too early. A few years later, he suffered an epileptic seizure on the field and was committed, penniless, to Cheadle Asylum where he died at the age of thirty-nine.'

Overall the 1894 season proved another fruitful one for Briggs with the ball (145 wickets at 13.83) and his batting proved useful too (675 runs at 19.28). He played in 21 of Lancashire's 23 first-class matches and in both of the prestige Gentlemen versus Players matches in London in July. He played in 15 championship matches and in first-class matches against Derbyshire and Leicestershire, outside that competition. In Lancashire's championship games, he and Mold were once again almost the only bowling resources employed. Between them the pair sent down 1,799 five-ball overs and took 241 wickets; twelve other bowlers bowled 466 overs and managed only 34 wickets, the best of them taking nine in all. Not surprisingly Lancashire were not in contention for the title, but they did tie their match with the champions, Surrey, at The Oval in mid-August. This was the only tied match played by Briggs in his long career, and *Wisden* described it as 'the sensational match of the London season'. Briggs took 13 wickets in the match, but had little involvement in its final overs as Lancashire's tail-enders struggled to reach 74 on a wet pitch against the might of Tom Richardson and Bill Lockwood, who weeks later were Briggs' teammates in Stoddart's side in Australia. At one point Lancashire, on 26 for 7, looked a beaten side, but Alfred Tinsley and wicket-keeper Charles Smith turned things round with the score progressing to 62 for 7 before the last three wickets went down for 12 runs.

The low point of Briggs' season was the way the fates – and in particular the Manchester weather – conspired against him during his benefit match, the long-awaited three-day Whitsuntide Bank Holiday game against Yorkshire at Old Trafford, starting on 14 May. There were 15,000 present at the scheduled start, but they were made to wait while the pitch was inspected. Because of the importance of the game, Lancashire had prepared two wickets, one of which had been covered by oil-sheets whenever there had been rain about; the other being left to the vagaries of the weather. Having looked at the covered wicket, Lord Hawke, the Yorkshire captain, objected to the surface. According to W.E.Howard, the Lancashire pavilion attendant, in his book 'Fifty Years' Cricket: Reminiscences of a Non-Player', published in 1928: 'When his lordship came into the dressing room after inspecting the ground, he remarked to me: 'I'm very sorry for Briggs, but I have come here to play county cricket and not for a benefit match'. Hawke wanted a new pitch to be made ready as quickly as possible, but many critics felt it would provide a similarly difficult surface for batting.

Hornby won the toss and chose to bat in front of a crowd which had by then grown to more than 22,000. In hindsight, it was the wrong decision. Lancashire, who started disastrously losing their first four wickets without scoring, were bowled out for 50 with only two men – one of them Briggs, obviously desperate to prolong proceedings – getting into double figures. Despite Briggs' best efforts with the ball – he took 5 for 62 –Yorkshire led by a more than useful 102 runs on first innings. Lancashire fell four runs short of making the visitors bat again, being bowled out for 98 and the match ended before lunch on the second day.

When Briggs came in to bat, the match had all but run away from Lancashire and Hawke, fielding at point, attempted to tell Briggs how sorry he was at the turn of events. Briggs famously retorted: 'I don't want to speak to you now my Lord.' It took Briggs a lot of persuading not to return to Hawke his donation of one guinea to the benefit fund. Despite Briggs' anger on the day, in later years he and Hawke, a man who was said never to hold a grudge, were very much on speaking terms. Hawke, although himself born in Lincolnshire, was nevertheless a fierce advocate of Yorkshire's 'born-in-the-county' policy. As a player and later as an administrator he was for more than 50 years one of the game's major figures. He captained Yorkshire for 28 seasons, during which time they won eight championships, and later served at various times as president, treasurer and trustee of MCC.

The early finish to the Yorkshire match was a financial body blow to Briggs, whose collection raised £1,000 when he must have been expecting close to double that amount. Briggs' Lancashire colleague Richard Pilling had taken his benefit in 1889 after 13 years' service behind the stumps and the sum of £1,500 was raised from a match between the North and South at Old Trafford in July. And, much to Briggs' chagrin, Peel's benefit, played less than three months after the Lancashire man's own benefit, the August Bank Holiday return match at Park Avenue, Bradford between Yorkshire and Lancashire, produced an even better return of almost £2,000.

There was a third clash between Lancashire and Yorkshire that season – a first-class match but outside the championship– at the Scarborough Festival, starting on 3 September, billed as XI of Yorkshire versus XI of Lancashire. Lord Hawke captained Yorkshire, but Briggs was not in the Lancashire line-up. Perhaps he didn't want another confrontation with his lordship so soon after their previous contretemps. There is no extant record of what Briggs had to say about missing this game although a perfectly innocent explanation might have been that he was getting ready to leave on Stoddart's tour to Australia, which was due to depart 15 days after the scheduled end of the festival fixture. There was controversy during the Scarborough match, when a tarpaulin was used to cover the pitch after the game had started, in contravention of Law 9, although Lord Hawke did not object. The cover was used so that spectators would not be disappointed by delays to play. Ironically, it proved insufficient to combat the east coast weather, and no cricket was possible on the third day.

As a footnote to this rather tumultuous season, Briggs played for Royton in the Central Lancashire League 'on his spare Saturdays' along with Barlow. But despite their efforts, Royton failed to land the championship that season. CLL clubs were allowed, until 1908, to engage two professionals although duties might include those of coach and groundsman.

Chapter Eleven
Touring with Stod

'No cricketer who ever lived was so much the child of nature as Briggs.'
Neville Cardus

The 1894/95 tourists, under the leadership of Stoddart, set sail for Australia from England on 21 September aboard the 6,814 ton *Ophir*. The ship belonged, like the *SS Orient*, to the Orient Line under its previous guise of the Orient Steam Navigation Company. They made one stop on the way at Colombo where they played a game on 16 October, in which Briggs had the locals in all sorts of trouble, taking 6 for 6. Briggs continued to be an automatic selection for tours even though, once again, the party consisted of only 13 players, including Peel, chosen more in the position of all-rounder than Briggs. Cricket was improving at a rate of knots down under and individual colony sides, encouraged perhaps by the Sheffield Shield competition, were much stronger and capable of taking on the tourists on an eleven-a-side basis. In all, Stoddart's side played 12 first-class matches, many on excellent pitches – a far cry from previous strips. Odds matches were played in far-flung country towns and though eleven of these were scheduled they were far less prevalent than on previous visits.

Stoddart was a late developer, not taking up the game seriously until he was 22. He was, however, a man of immeasurable stamina, scoring 485 in 370 minutes for Hampstead against the Stoics – at the time a world individual record – and all this after spending the entire night before the match playing poker. But that wasn't the end of his activities – he spent the rest of the afternoon playing tennis and rounded off the day with a dinner party that evening! He led England on two of his four tours to Australia becoming the first captain to put Australia in and the first to declare an England innings closed. But as he grew older his health began to deteriorate and he found it hard to come to terms with his growing physical frailties. In his later years he was also burdened by financial problems and he shot himself three weeks after his 52nd birthday.

It was during the course of this series that cricket really began to capture the public's imagination in Australia and crowds grew steadily during the series, culminating in an attendance of 29,000 for the Saturday of the Fifth Test in Melbourne, contributing to an overall five-day figure of almost 100,000 spectators. Interest was heightened by the fact that this was the first series comprehensively covered via the telegraph. In Sydney large crowds were said to have waited outside newspaper offices to read reports of each over about ten minutes after it had been bowled. These crowds would have read the exciting over-by-over dispatches as Briggs became a key component in England's famous 10-run win at Sydney in the First Test.

Australia had mauled England's attack in their first innings, reaching 586 all out, midway through the second day – echoes here of England's first innings of 551 in the Second Test at Adelaide on the 2006/07 tour which the visitors contrived to lose by the remarkable margin of six wickets. At Sydney, Briggs was powerless to prevent the Australians running riot, conceding 96 runs and going wicketless in 25 dispiriting overs. Australia's George Giffen (161) and Syd Gregory (201) gorged themselves on the England bowling, digging their side out of a deep hole at 21 for 3. Briggs did better with the bat, scoring a half century as England reached 325 although they failed to avoid the follow-on. In their second knock, England did even better, scoring 437 with Ward compiling a century as England gave themselves an outside chance of victory.

By the close of day five, the Australians on 113 for 2 seemed to be moving fairly serenely towards their modest victory target of 177. But they had reckoned without heavy overnight rain which turned the pitch into a genuine 'sticky dog' and gave Peel and Briggs just the sort of encouragement they needed. Early on, though, Australia had advanced to 130 for 2 only 47 runs away from victory. But then Peel and Briggs began to get into their stride and by the time England had wrapped up victory, eight wickets had fallen on the final day for 53 runs, with the last five going down for just eight. Peel finished with 6 for 67 and Briggs' return was 3 for 25.

During the course of the Fourth Test, also at Sydney, Briggs became the first bowler to claim 100 Test wickets – in his 25th Test – but achieving that milestone failed to stop Australia winning by an innings.

Briggs didn't excel in the other Tests in the five-match series which England won 3-2 and his batting rarely brought him many runs despite the fact that he was pushed up the order several times – in the Second Test he opened with MacLaren although the experiment wasn't a success, Briggs scoring only 12. Nevertheless, Briggs had been an integral part of the 'Ashes-winning' team celebrated by *Punch* magazine's famous poetic tribute, which contained the following lines:

> 'Then wrote the queen of England;
> Whose hand is blessed by God;
> I must do something handsome;
> For my dear victorious Stod.'

Chapter Twelve
Bowling Lancashire to their first official title

'No better all-round man than Briggs, to sustain his form for so long, has ever represented us, and no one is known better all over the world.' – A.N. 'Monkey' Hornby

Stoddart's tourists returned to Tilbury in early May 1895, again aboard the *Ophir*. They received a welcome almost as emotional as the farewell afforded them by a flotilla of small boats and well-wishers on the shoreline as the Ophir had pulled away from her moorings on a rainy day in Adelaide six weeks earlier. While they were abroad English first-class cricket had undergone a major transformation. Arising from various meetings during the winter, the county championship had been expanded from nine to 14 clubs, with the introduction or reintroduction of Derbyshire, Essex, Hampshire, Leicestershire and Warwickshire. The leading sides, including Lancashire, had organised 20 or more fixtures in the competition. This meant that their professionals had more or less full-time employment, playing cricket, from the beginning of May to the end of August. Many of the minor representative fixtures, which had once provided a major chunk of Briggs' playing season, had disappeared. It meant there were fewer opportunities for amateurs to play in occasional matches, and wickets became much harder to take. The scale of change can be seen in Lancashire's own returns in the championship. In 1894, the county scored 4,721 runs at 19.11 and took 279 wickets at 15.33 in the competition. However, in 1895, they scored 7,838 runs at 23.60 and took 385 wickets at 16.30. By the turn of the century the leading counties expected their batsmen to score 10,000 championship runs, and their bowlers to take 400 wickets in the competition, costing around 25 runs apiece.

Above all else the season of 1895 was the year of W.G.Grace. He scored 2,346 first-class runs and compiled nine centuries, including his 'hundredth hundred'. Even though he had not taken part in the tour, Grace's 'hundredth hundred' intruded on Stoddart's side's celebration dinner at the Café Monico in Piccadilly in late May. Briggs bowled against Grace in four matches during the season, but secured his wicket only twice, once when he had scored 104. Lancashire finished second in the championship, rather better than many had expected. Once more, they relied heavily on the bowling of Mold and Briggs, who took 182 and 119 wickets respectively. They had, however, secured the services of Albert Hallam, a Nottingham-born right-arm medium pace bowler, who in 14 matches shared some of the burden. By now the appearances of MacLaren, Lancashire's appointed captain, were also irregular. At Taunton, he returned on 15 July to lead the side after missing the county's six previous matches, and scored the first ever quadruple century in first-class cricket. MacLaren feasted on the Somerset bowling – everyone but the wicketkeeper was called upon to bowl – and, in truth, Somerset fielded a

Lancashire line-up 1895:
Briggs (cross-legged on the ground, as usual, front left) with his team mates,
Charles Smith, Aldred Tinsley (both seated).
Back row: Arthur Mold, Albert Paul, Samuel Lunt (scorer), George Baker,
Arthur Smith.
Middle row: Albert Ward, Sidney Tindall, Archie MacLaren (captain),
Gerald Bardswell, Frank Sugg.

below-strength team, containing nine amateurs, including a doctor and a vicar. The latter couldn't provide any divine intervention, particularly when MacLaren had reached 'only' 262 with Henry Stanley failing to cling on to a very difficult chance from a full-blooded drive to mid-on. He offered another chance when past 400 – a vicious straight drive off one of Lionel Palairet's lobs. During the course of his marathon effort, MacLaren and Arthur Paul put on 363 for the second wicket, advancing the score from 141 for 1 to 504 for 2. When MacLaren was finally caught in the deep with the score on 792, Briggs came to the wicket and, scoring all Lancashire's last nine runs, took the total past 800 for the first time in county cricket history. When Somerset batted, he and Mold swept away the demoralised opposition twice for 143 and 206, taking nine wickets each.

Briggs' own batting in this season was distinctly modest. For the first time since 1882 he failed to score a fifty, and by the end the season was regularly going in at eight or nine. He did not play in either of the Gentlemen versus Players matches in London, with Peel taking the place he might have filled. He was, however, reunited with his colleagues from Stoddart's side that had toured Australia in festival matches at Hastings, playing before 'vast crowds' in the final fixtures of the season. Apart from helping England to that remarkable win at Sydney, Briggs' form on that 1894/95 tour wasn't exactly sparkling, but there were no signs that his bowling was on the wane in the domestic arena and in the 1895 season he captured 124 wickets at 15.46.

The Australians were in England in 1896, playing 34 matches, all of them first-class although, in truth, some were modest affairs. The three-match Test series was won 2-1 by England. Briggs played six games against the tourists, two of them for Lancashire, but in only one Test. This was at Manchester where, of course, the side was selected by the county. In that match, which Australia won, he took three wickets and scored 16 runs, which by his own high standards was a modest performance. It was clear that at 33, he could no longer lay claim to an automatic Test place.

However, he played two matches a week, more or less every week, so that he appeared in 30 first-class matches in the season, more than in any other season in his career. He bowled 1,781 five-ball overs, easily his biggest seasonal total. Only the Middlesex and England right-arm medium pace bowler Jack Hearne bowled more overs, but he was rewarded with almost a hundred more wickets than Briggs. Briggs' ability to take wickets seems to have fallen away. In one extreme example, he bowled 90 five-ball overs, taking 6 for 185, against Derbyshire, who scored 577 at Old Trafford in August when Mold was away playing in a Test. Briggs played in all 22 championship matches for Lancashire, who made a sustained challenge for the title, at one stage early in the season winning eight consecutives matches. But with only three regular bowlers, Briggs, Hallam and Mold, they were not as strong an outfit as their cross-Pennine rivals, Yorkshire, who won both Roses matches and the championship.

Although Briggs' bowling skills appeared to be on the decline in 1896, he confounded his critics the following season when his skill with the ball helped Lancashire win a close-run championship by the shortest of short heads from Surrey. Lancashire headed the table on 14 August, but Surrey were closing fast and the two teams met in what was being billed as a championship decider at The Oval, starting on 19 August. Interest was high and on the first day's play 30,000 were present to see Richardson turn the match for the London-based side on a treacherous wicket drying under the late summer sun. Lancashire found themselves 62 behind on first innings and ended the second day on 112 for 6 in their second innings. The visitors had no answer to the fiery Richardson, who in murky conditions, laid out MacLaren, broke Ward's bat, broke both Ward's bat and his finger, injured Radcliffe and hit Briggs three painful blows. Johnny Tyldesley faced one over from the fast bowler in which every delivery whizzed over his head. Lancashire succumbed by six wickets with Richardson claiming 11 victims, and it looked as though the title had slipped from Lancashire's grasp, especially as they could only draw their next game against Middlesex at Lord's.

In those days the title was decided by subtracting defeats from wins, ignoring all drawn matches, with the final order being decided by the percentage of points gained from completed matches. It meant that if a team won only one match and drew all its other games it would have a percentage of 100 and would win the title! Lancashire started their final game against Nottinghamshire at Old Trafford on 26 August, the same day that Surrey were due to begin their game against Somerset at Taunton. Lancashire won by an innings giving them a percentage of 68.42, but all Surrey had to do to stay ahead of them was to avoid defeat in the West Country and in their final match against Sussex. But the form book went out of the window at Taunton and Somerset beat Surrey to record only their third win of the season. The Sussex game at Hove became academic – it ended in a draw with Sussex in a fairly strong position when rain intervened and prevented any play on the final day – and after starting the final two games with a percentage of 70, Surrey ended the season on 61.90 and had to settle for the runner-up spot, despite having beaten Lancashire twice. It was the first time Lancashire had finished on top in the official competition.

Briggs' bowling was a key factor in Lancashire's success. He was the county's leading wicket taker with 140 at 16.38 and finished second in the championship bowling averages. He was helped by the fact that for the first time in several campaigns, Lancashire were able to avail themselves of the services of four regular bowlers with Briggs and Mold being augmented by Hallam and Willis Cuttell, then aged 32, a slow right-armer from Nelson. The latter pair did their fair share of the work, bowling more than 900 overs, capturing 90 and 102 wickets respectively.

Briggs came to the fore when the pressure was on – as was his wont. He held the Lancashire bowling together when Mold was injured, taking 25 wickets in the last four games for a Lancashire side which was badly handicapped by injuries which kept wicket-keeper Smith and batsman Frank Sugg out of the team for a time.

But for all his accuracy, Briggs did have occasional off days and against Sussex at Manchester in July he came in for a fearful hammering in both innings. Mold was away playing in a Test match, so Briggs sent down 66 five-ball overs in the first innings and another 60 in the second. But he went almost unrewarded. He took 2 for 174 in 66 overs in the first innings and returned 2 for 132 in 60 overs when Sussex batted a second time. Despite the punishment he was receiving, Lancashire captain MacLaren kept Briggs on for over after unproductive over. The situation descended into such farce that the crowd cheered ironically every time Briggs walked up to start a fresh over. One newspaper commented: 'To the jollying of the crowd, he [MacLaren] was as impervious as a stone wall; ironical cheering whenever he fielded a ball had no effect. Altogether the affair resolved itself into a demonstration of cheap dignity on the part of the Lancashire captain in which he was the solitary loser.' Another newspaper dubbed MacLaren, who compounded the felony by dropping his

Sussex opposite number, K.S.Ranjitsinhji, twice on his way to 87, as 'Haughty Archibald'. The *City News* said of MacLaren: 'A petulant obstinacy which he seems to mistake for firmness occasionally distorts his judgement.' The match ended in a draw but it did provide Briggs with a Lancashire county record – almost certainly unwanted – that of the most balls bowled in a match with his 126 five-ball overs adding up to 630 deliveries. Three years later, Briggs came pretty close to beating his own record when he sent down 606 deliveries in the match against Kent at Manchester. This time he was marginally more successful, taking six wickets from 101 six-ball overs. Once again Briggs' efforts failed to produce a result, the game ending in a draw.

Next stop for Briggs was Stoddart's 1897/88 trip to Australia. It was to be his last tour – and his inclusion probably owed a little to the exclusion of Peel, who upset his captain Lord Hawke at Yorkshire by his intemperate behaviour, coming on to the field in a drunken state after what was presumably a liquid lunch on the third day of the home match against Middlesex at Sheffield. But Briggs was, in fact, the leading bowler playing with the leading county, so perhaps Peel's aberration made little difference. Peel was to play little first-class cricket in the wake of the Sheffield incident. Briggs himself was chosen purely for his bowling and not as an all-rounder – there were three all-rounders in the side all of whom had completed the double in the domestic season just ended – and the Lancashire man rarely batted above eight and sometimes as low as ten.

The outstanding success of Stoddart's tour of 1894/95 had encouraged the Melbourne Cricket Club to promote this second tour, which left Tilbury on 17 October, 1897. Stoddart plainly liked touring: he was member of Lord Hawke's side to the West Indies in 1896/97, and attracted as much attention there as he had in Australia three years earlier. Incidentally, the West Indies tour motto was TWBF, 'There Will Be Fun', although, by now, some critics were beginning to question Stoddart's amateur status.

The side played 22 matches in all, so this was perhaps the least arduous of all Briggs' six Australian tours. Twelve were of first-class status, of which five were Test matches, and there were ten matches against odds, mostly in various towns and cities away from the colonial capitals. After the tourists had won the First Test match, Australia won the remaining four, two of them by an innings. *Wisden* said of the tour: 'There has not for a very long time been anything so disappointing in connection with English cricket ...'

For Briggs, the tour was just as disappointing and was to provide a sad footnote to his Test touring career. His top score was 46 not out in the Second Test, during which the Australian batsman Charlie McLeod, who was deaf, was 'bowled'. A no-ball was called, but McLeod unaware of the umpire's shout, began to walk back to the pavilion. England wicket-keeper Bill Storer spotted that McLeod was out of his crease threw the stumps down and McLeod was adjudged run out! Never let it be said that poor sportsmanship is a modern malaise. McLeod made amends with 112 in the next Test as Australia completed the first innings win in Test history.

That 46 apart, Briggs failed with the bat time and again. He batted in a variety of positions and was even tried as an opener in the Fourth Test at Melbourne where he didn't let the side down altogether, scoring 23. He only reached double figures on four other occasions in first-class matches during the visit. But if his batting was poor, his bowling was virtually impotent. He took only nine wickets in the five Tests with his best figures of 3 for 96 in the second match of the series at Melbourne and ended with only 14 first-class wickets in total. He came in for plenty of stick, returning very uncharacteristic figures of 1 for 128 in the third Test at Adelaide and 2 for 98 and 1 for 101 against New South Wales at Sydney. He played in only eight first-class matches although he was neither ill nor injured, fewer games than all but Stoddart himself, who was sick for part of the tour. In the games Briggs missed, the reserve wicket-keeper Jack Board, was drafted in. Even in odds matches, where in the past Briggs would have been expected to cause mayhem against the less technically adept local batsmen, he was a failure, taking only 45 wickets with a best of 9 for 84 in an innings against a Bendigo XVIII. He didn't play in the final two first-class matches as the tour wound down. It was clearly a tour too far for Briggs.

Perhaps his almost non-stop schedule had caught up with him at last; Lancashire certainly didn't spare him. Or perhaps he was just out of sorts for the duration of the tour. After all, he had been on five previous trips to Australia and maybe the novelty value had worn off. Who knows, but maybe Briggs' singularly poor form may have resonated far beyond the boundary. In *The Bulletin*, a heavyweight Australian periodical, an article published on 18 March, 1898, opined: 'This ruthless rout of English cricket will do –

and has done – more to the Australian nationality than could ever be achieved by miles of erudite essays and impassioned appeal.' The Commonwealth of Australia became a reality in 1901 – and they have been ruthless ever since, at least on the cricket pitch, and usually against England!

Chapter Thirteen
Slipping alarmingly

'With a wicket to help him he could be a terror. He was a cheery, podgy soul, full of humour who perhaps played a little to the gallery, but never gave anything away.' Lord Hawke

In the wake of the tour, the 1898 domestic season saw Briggs' form slip alarmingly with both bat and ball. He scored 507 runs at an average of only 16.90 and failed to hit three figures as a wicket-taker with only 80 victims at a much higher rate than was his norm – 24.17. More alarmingly, in Lancashire's last 12 matches, Briggs took only 24 wickets at an inflated average of 38.16. They finished sixth of 14 in the championship. Lancashire's bowling attack was badly hit by injuries and illness, especially the season-long absence, through pneumonia, of Hallam.

The situation was so desperate that the committee took the unusual step of asking Alec Watson, then 51 and having been retired for five years, to help them out. Wise counsel prevailed and Scottish-born Watson turned down the request. Watson did, however, turn out for Buckinghamshire seven years later! He was by then 59 and played his sole game against Bedfordshire at Osborne Street, Wolverton. He wasn't a success, taking 2 for 104 in 35 overs and scoring four and two, batting at No.11. He bowled Rev R.H.Moss and caught and bowled the Bedfordshire professional George Wharmby, who played six matches for Lancashire and also played for Nottinghamshire. Buckinghamshire went down to a heavy defeat, losing by an innings and 61 runs.

Because of his poor form, he wasn't invited to play in the 'big match' of the season, the Gentlemen v Players game at Lord's in July, which was arranged to coincide with W.G.Grace's fiftieth birthday. At the end of the season he did play two further matches, both at the Hastings Festival, one of which was a reunion for Stoddart's Australian side, but he contributed little in either game.

Chapter Fourteen
Seizure at the Music Hall

'Tell the public I am all right.' Johnny Briggs

Briggs played in only 13 first-class matches for Lancashire in 1899, the year he suffered his seizure in June. He wasn't having a particularly good season with either bat or ball, claiming just 57 wickets at 19.24 for the county and scoring 284 runs in 20 innings for an average of 16.70. He rarely proved a match-winner with the ball in a disappointing championship season for Lancashire, who finished fourth in the competition. But his best all-round performance came at an opportune time, when his selection for the Third Test against the Australians at Headingley was under the spotlight. The match in question was against Yorkshire at Sheffield, where Briggs did his Test prospects no harm at all with ten wickets and two useful innings.

Nevertheless, his place in the England side was in doubt right up to the morning of the match. He had been championed by his county captain MacLaren, who knew how desperate Briggs was to complete 100 Test wickets against Australia, but the *Leeds Evening Express* reported that Briggs ultimately 'took the eleventh place in the side'. In fact, the day before the Test was due to start, the proceedings at Sheffield were interrupted several times, even though the game was delicately poised, by the appearance on the field of Yorkshire captain Lord Hawke, who wished to consult with MacLaren about the composition of the Test team. In the end, Briggs replaced Yorkshire's young Wilfred Rhodes, who was to become one of the game's greatest all-rounders with more than 40,000 runs and in excess of 4,000 wickets in a career that spanned 37 seasons. Originally, Stanley Jackson had said he wanted to be left out, but the Yorkshireman changed his mind and indicated he wanted to play, so it was decided to omit Tom Hayward and play his Surrey colleague Bill Brockwell along with Briggs. However, Brockwell damaged a hand and his team-mate Hayward was back in the side.

Of course, Briggs never made it to the magic century. He was taken ill after the first day's play having increased his tally to 97 by capturing three wickets and never appeared in another Test. Briggs did well on the first day on 29 June, 1899, taking 3 for 53 from his 30 five-ball overs as the visitors were restricted to an all-out total of 172 in their first innings. The *Leeds Evening Express* reported that Briggs was 'in wonderful form'. By the close, the match was evenly poised with England on 119 for 4. Unfortunately, rain wiped out the final day's play with England on 19 for 0, chasing 177 for what would have been a series-levelling victory.

England had, of course, to make do without Briggs for the rest of the match. He went into the scorebook as 'absent ill' in their first innings and although he didn't know it, he was never to play at the highest level again. Later on that first day, Briggs and some of his colleagues went on a night out to the Empire Palace music hall on Briggate in Leeds, which was considered to be one of the finest in the country. It staged its opening performances only ten months before the Headingley Test after being built in an area of Leeds between Briggate and Vicar Lane, which had been redeveloped by the Leeds Estate Company. The theatre seated 1,750 in three tiers and the audience certainly received value for money on the opening night on 29 August, 1898 when 17 acts were served up for their delectation, including Lydia Yeamens, the original 'Sally in our Alley', Harry Tate and John Higgins, who was billed as 'The Human Kangaroo'. Later major stars like Charlie Chaplin and Vesta Tilley appeared on the Empire stage and in the 1950s top-of-the bill artistes included the Beverley Sisters, Joan Regan, Tommy Trinder, Dickie Valentine, Harry Secombe, Frankie Vaughan and Cliff Richard. The curtain came down for the final time on 25 February, 1961 after a performance of Babes in the Wood, starring Nat Jackley, and the theatre is now the site of the Harvey Nicholls department store, part of a busy pedestrian-only shopping street.

The night Briggs and some of his England colleagues visited the Empire Palace, the entertainment was billed as being 'under the Special Patronage and in the Presence of the Australian and English cricket teams' according to the theatre's own advertisement in that night's *Leeds Evening Express*. Bunting was strung around the outside of the theatre and the lights were full on, picking out the crowds as they arrived. Over the main entrance was a stretch of canvas bearing a single word 'Welcome'. Appearing on the bill that fateful night were Ludwig Amman, an impersonator who took on the personas of both Emile Zola and Captain Dreyfus, and the actress and singer Millie Hylton, who was also an impersonator. She was best known for her impersonations of 'giddy young men addicted to the practice of painting the town red'. Not surprisingly, with players from England and Australia in the audience, the theatre was packed to the rafters despite the counter-attractions of several other Leeds' theatres, including the Grand Theatre, the Theatre Royal, the New Queen's Theatre and the Tivoli Theatre of Varieties, all of whom were vying for patronage that evening. Seats in the Grand Circle at the Empire Palace and many of the stage boxes were set aside for the two teams and their guests.

The cricketers began to arrive at about nine o'clock and many of them were given an enthusiastic greeting by the audience. But at about 10.15pm the mood was to change dramatically when Briggs, who was in the front row and had been chatting to a member of the Australian team, suddenly threw up his arms and collapsed. He was carried unconscious into the foyer and was later taken by taxi to the home of a Mr Bagshaw, one of the vice-presidents of the Leeds Cricket Club. Few in the theatre knew what was going on and the performance continued. By now, though, Briggs was being attended to by a Dr Iredale who decided, understandably, that Briggs could take no further part in the match. Iredale stayed with Briggs throughout the night, during which time he was reported to have suffered several more seizures, and wired Mrs Briggs about the serious condition of her husband.

The next day Briggs was taken by train across the Pennines to Exchange Station in Manchester where he was met by a representative of Cheadle Lunatic Asylum in Heald Green, Cheshire. Clearly disorientated, all Briggs could manage to say was: 'Tell the public I am all right.' Cheadle asylum was built between 1847 and 1849 as 'a private asylum for the middle and upper classes'. It stood on a site which was part of Finney Farm on Long Lane and from the outside it looked like a large Victorian mansion. Author Joseph Connolly, in his book, 'The Treatment of the Insane without Mechanical Constraint', had earlier described the asylum, set in open countryside about eight miles from the centre of Manchester, as 'a building with spacious grounds opening on to gardens and windows commanding agreeable views'.

Inside the asylum, the reality might have been somewhat different. In the final year of the nineteenth century, epilepsy, commonly known as the 'the falling sickness', usually meant removal either to a lunatic asylum or the workhouse. Sufferers were, by and large, stigmatized. The general public of 100 years ago believed that epilepsy was a mental illness. There was a feeling that with the right treatment patients could be cured of their epilepsy, but another reason for their confinement was as a protection for themselves and for the public at large, particularly if they were susceptible to regular seizures. The proportion of asylum patients with epilepsy might have been as high as 20 per cent and soon the medical authorities began to press not only for special epileptic wards but for separate institutions. By the late 1890s, when Briggs was confined, treatment of epilepsy was becoming more sophisticated. Older methods, including dosing with metallic salts and applying threads under the skin, blisters and cupping were gradually being phased out. Instead, Briggs would probably have been treated with bromide salts, especially potassium bromide although the side effects of such treatments included lethargy, muscle weakness and purulent acne.

It is probable that while Briggs was having an epileptic fit he would have been isolated in a padded cell and would have had to wear a skull cap to protect his head. However, there are reports that occasionally during his stay in the asylum Briggs played cricket in the hospital grounds against a Manchester side led by his former Lancashire captain 'Monkey' Hornby and scored a number of centuries. It is also said that Briggs bowled long spells down the hospital corridors, afterwards regaling the medical staff with details of his 'figures'. So it is likely that Briggs either didn't fall

Another Lancashire player, Jim Hallows, was to succumb to epilepsy. Hallows, an all-rounder who like Briggs bowled slow left-arm, was only 36 when he passed away. In 1904 he became only the second Lancashire player after Willis Cuttell to achieve the double of 1,000 runs and 100 wickets in a season. His performances were recognised by *Wisden* who made him one of their cricketers of the year in 1905. Hallows joined the Old Trafford staff in 1897 and made his debut the following year, but he was far from robust and missed several games through ill-health. He had an epileptic seizure during the 1905 Roses match at Old Trafford and had to be carried from the field by Cuttell and Lees Radcliffe.

prey to these debilitating side effects or was treated instead with other older remedies that might have included zinc and arsenic compounds.

But the age-old treatment of purging for epilepsy did survive the various changes in the way the illness was treated. If that was the case it must have been an awful experience for the stricken Briggs as purging consisted of vomiting, inappropriate use of laxatives, enemas, diuretics or other medication. It might have also consisted of excessive physical exercise or fasting. It speaks volumes for Briggs' constitution that he was able to come through all this relatively unscathed and was, in fact, discharged from his doctors' care after almost eight months on 28 March, 1900.

Amazingly, just five weeks later – on 7 May – Briggs was back in action, playing for Lancashire in their opening championship match against Hampshire at Old Trafford, only a few days after proving his fitness in a warm-up match for A.N.Hornby's XI against Levenshulme. He was given a warm welcome back by the home supporters and scored 19 and 29, but wasn't called upon to bowl by Lancashire's captain MacLaren, who relied on Cuttell and Sidney Webb, who took 19 Hampshire wickets between them – the other dismissal was a run out – as Lancashire got off to the best possible start to the new campaign with a 265-run victory. Strangely this match had not appeared on the original list of fixtures drawn up at the annual meeting of club secretaries at Lord's and no umpires had been appointed by the game's ruling body. Instead, two members of the Lancashire ground staff stood on the first day.

Briggs must have had an iron constitution as he played in 27 matches for Lancashire that year, scoring 761 runs at a slightly reduced average of 20.56 with a highest score of 58 not out. But illness and his confinement in the asylum had not appeared to diminish Briggs' bowling talents and he ended the season with haul of 120 victims – more than double his total in the previous year – at an average of 17.45. Even his fielding still attracted attention: Digby Jephson, who captained Surrey between 1900 and 1902 and was one of the game's last lob bowlers, singled him out in an article in the 1901 *Wisden*, referring to his work at cover point as 'nearly as good as it ever was'.

It was a remarkable comeback and the highlight of his season came as early as the fourth match. After the win over Hampshire, Lancashire completed easy victories over Derbyshire at Old

Trafford, and Warwickshire at Liverpool, and were playing their fourth successive home game when they took on Worcestershire at Old Trafford, starting on 24 May. According to MacLaren, the wicket was 'a trifle soft on top but firm underneath, and which steadily improved under a drying wind with very little sun'. The crowd, which numbered 7,000 on the first day, was in good heart, celebrating that day the 81st birthday of Queen Victoria. The Worcestershire captain Harry Foster – one of seven brothers all of whom played for the county – decided to bat first. MacLaren felt that winning the toss was neither here nor there and wasn't particularly perturbed when Foster called correctly.

Soon Briggs had the visitors in a spin and Worcestershire were quickly 6 for 3. By lunchtime Briggs had taken the first seven wickets and throughout the interval the crowd was wondering whether Briggs would become the eighth player to take all ten and the second Lancashire player to achieve the feat. He assured his captain that he would do it to celebrate the Queen's birthday, but for a while it didn't look as though he would.

And there was audible displeasure from the home crowd when Mold and Cuttell each came close to taking a wicket. Briggs returned to the attack, but Albert Bird and Robert Burrows batted with more confidence than any of their team-mates and it looked as though Briggs might be denied. Gradually, though, Briggs worked his way through the remaining batsmen, clean bowling both Burrows and Bird. The final wicket came off the penultimate ball of Briggs 29th over and his analysis in the scorebook read: 28.5-7-55-10. Briggs took 3 for 62 in Worcestershire's second innings as Lancashire completed a five-wicket win.

As MacLaren recalled: 'The last wicket took a lot of getting, but when Bird, who played the best cricket of the lot, jumped out to drive, and then hesitating missed the ball in playing back, and the ball hit the sticks, Johnny's bashful smile as he turned round for his sweater was well worth seeing.' 'It was all the more creditable owing to the fact that wicket was never difficult. He has on two previous occasions taken nine wickets, once against the Australians at Scarborough, when the last man was run out, but this was the first occasion on which he has taken the lot. Johnny we are proud of you.' MacLaren's memory must have been playing tricks with him as Briggs had taken nine in an innings on three occasions, recording 9 for 29 against Derbyshire at Derby in 1885, and 9 for 88 against Sussex at Old Trafford, 1888, in addition to capturing nine Australian wickets for 31 at Scarborough in 1890 when appearing for Lord Londesborough's XI.

Briggs had equalled the 'all ten' accomplished by Lancashire's Chesterfield-born fast bowler William Hickton almost 30 years before in the match against Hampshire, also at Old Trafford. Hickton, whose figures were a county record 10 for 46, played in only 24 matches for Lancashire between 1867 and 1871 before joining his native county, Derbyshire, for whom he played a further 34 games between 1871 and 1878. The only other Red Rose bowler to bowl out an entire side was Bob Berry and again Worcestershire were the fall guys. Berry, a left-arm slow bowler like Briggs, and who died in December 2006 at the age of 80, took 10 for 102 at Blackpool in Coronation year, 1953. Berry played twice for England, taking nine wickets on his debut match in 1950 against the West Indies on a spin-friendly Old Trafford surface. But he found it difficult to hold down a regular place in the Lancashire side and joined Worcestershire, where had three of his most successful seasons. He ended his career at Derbyshire, joining them in 1958 and thus became the first man to be capped by three counties.

After his 'all ten', Briggs took his good form into the next match, against Middlesex at Lord's, ending with 7 for 87 in the Middlesex first innings to set up another Lancashire win. He scored two fifties against Kent to add to his six wickets but didn't play against Yorkshire at Park Avenue, Bradford, returning to take 5 for 60 against Nottinghamshire at Trent Bridge and then 5-35 against Middlesex at Old Trafford. And he continued his impressive run with the ball with 4 for 9 as Somerset were bowled out for 40 at Aigburth and 6 for 95 against Warwickshire at Edgbaston. Lancashire were in contention for the championship for most of the season, but ultimately failed in their quest for top spot. Surprisingly, Briggs was promoted up the order to open the innings against Leicestershire at Grace Road and he didn't let the Red Rose down, scoring 43. Even more surprisingly, he donned the wicket-keeper's gloves in the closing stages of this match as it ebbed away to a draw to allow Charles Smith to bowl the only four overs of his Lancashire career. Smith, who even managed a wicket, had, in fact, opened the innings with Briggs on the first day. The Leeds-born keeper played 168 times for Lancashire in ten seasons, bagging 437 victims (318 caught; 119 stumped). But despite his rare batting 'promotion', Briggs was still winning matches with the ball, taking nine wickets against Derbyshire at the North Road Ground, Glossop and 7 for 53 and 3 for 22 against Nottinghamshire at Old Trafford.

In what proved to be his 391st and last first-class appearance for Lancashire before his death, Briggs contributed with both bat and ball in the home match against Leicestershire, hitting 36 not out in his only innings and taking 2 for 41 in the first innings and 6 for 49 on the final afternoon – his last afternoon of cricket at Old Trafford – on 1 September, 1900. Lancashire were also indebted to their openers, MacLaren, who scored a quickfire second innings 145 and Leeds-born Albert Ward who scored a painstaking 120, batting four hours and 20 minutes in the first innings. Fittingly, though, it was Briggs who applied the finishing touches with his six wickets in 23 deadly accurate overs as Leicestershire collapsed to 120 all out, giving Lancashire a 260-run victory, even though play had been delayed until 2.45 on the final afternoon. Thus Briggs had ended the last of his 22 seasons for Lancashire, the side he had loved and served with such devotion, with 761 first-class runs at 20.56 and 120 wickets at 17.45. Once again, Briggs had finished as the side's leading bowler, eleven ahead of Cuttell.

After the usual festival matches at Scarborough and Hastings had been played, MCC organised a benefit match on 14, 15 and 16 September for Philip Need, one of the club's long serving pavilion attendants, between the North of England and the South of England. The match, played at Lord's twelve days after Lancashire had completed their win over Leicestershire, attracted many of the leading players of the time, including W.G.Grace, Stoddart, Plum Warner, Hayward, Gilbert Jessop, Albert Trott, Lord Hawke, Hirst and Rhodes. Briggs also played. It was to be the last match of his career. But he bowed out with 6 for 135 in the first innings and 1 for 25 in the second. Briggs' fifth wicket in that first innings – Jephson for one – chalked up what was to prove the last milestone in a career full of milestones, the two-hundredth occasion on which he had taken five in an innings in a first-class match. He became the second cricketer, behind the great man himself, W.G.Grace, to achieve that feat. In the North's second innings, Jephson repaid the compliment, bowling Briggs for 18, the last runs he ever made in first-class cricket.

Few who had either played with or watched Briggs in action that season would have expected it to be his last, although Dr Scowcroft said that throughout the summer, as well as he played,

Briggs was never himself, while the *Manchester Guardian* wrote: 'Those who frequently saw him noted the unhappy difference between the Briggs of old and the new Briggs of 1900.

Chapter Fifteen
What are we to make of him?

'It's not what ah do, it's what t'others think ah do as matters.' Johnny Briggs

So what are we to make of Johnny Briggs? It is both futile and fallacious to compare sportsman across the generations. What we do know is that Briggs was one of the most popular players to have graced the game. He was truly a working-class hero. Coming from humble beginnings he had made it to the very top of his chosen profession. The fans, largely working class themselves, were able to identify with him. I wasn't fortunate enough to see Briggs perform, so perhaps it might be best left to Neville Cardus, one of the greatest writers on the game, to tell the reader what Briggs was all about. Although Cardus was only 11 when he first saw Briggs play, in 1900 at the tail-end of his career, he seems, like the prescient observer that he was, to have captured much of the essence of the player.

Cardus himself came from a poor Manchester family and had little formal education so there was a certain symmetry between the two men. After doing some cricket coaching and spending some time as secretary to the headmaster at Shrewsbury School, Cardus, who had been rejected for military service, went into journalism with the *Manchester Guardian* where he remained for the rest of his working life apart from a spell in Australia between 1939 and 1947. In 1970, Cardus was elected president of Lancashire. He wrote equally well and perceptively about music as he did about cricket.

In Briggs, Cardus saw something of the sad clown figure of Joseph Grimaldi suggesting that Briggs might not always have been as happy on the inside as he looked on the outside. Cardus obviously developed a deep love for Briggs the cricketer and wrote of him in his book 'Days in the Sun'.

'He was surely born for the game, for he was a sort of little indiarubber ball of a man, and he seemingly remained in one position more than a second at a time only by strong will-power.'

'When he walked from the pavilion at Old Trafford (under his arm that mummy of a bat of his, in the ancient binding) one had the notion that if he came down too heavily on the turf he would bounce back again into the dressing room through the window.'

'Recollect how he went to the wicket. He was, one thought, like a happy boy going for a walk or rather in quest of adventure. His eyes shone humour at you; his every movement was alive, and youthfully alive.'

'One has known dull days and dull cricket before the advent of Briggs, but he had just to show his face and a light passed over the field, and with it companionable warmth.'

'He was a man into whose body the humours of summer entered day by day – sunshine, wind and refreshing dews.'

'No cricketer who ever lived was so much the child of nature as Briggs.'

'This man a subtle bowler? you might well have asked, looking at his bland eyes, yet he was a very Heathen Chinee of cricket. He bowled you a left-handed ball with a quite casual motion; his arm swept over almost ingratiatingly. His run to the wicket was modest, and a little mincing. But if the turf were at all susceptible to spin, the ball he sent you had a bottle imp inside it. It might twist so viciously that a little tuft of grass was cut from the pitch; it might scuttle to the base of your stumps like a mouse; it might jump up at you and rap your knuckles abominably.'

'Yet it was hard to be short with him despite his deceit. He was a child playing tricks with you. When he bowled you neck and crop there was a cocky little strut in his walk as he moved to mid-off to tell him exactly how the ball had pitched on your legs and hit your off wicket. And again it was hard to be short with him. Obviously he had bowled you in sheer fun; you simply had to join in the general laughter.'

But Cardus, who was knighted in 1967, added: 'There is in the eyes a look of a man not born to be funny from morning till night, day in and day out. The old tragedy of the comedian, indeed, was in Briggs.'

Another man whose opinion one must respect in regard to Briggs' merit was the legend himself – W.G.Grace. With 54,000 runs spread over 44 seasons and 2,800-plus wickets costing less than 18 each, no one is more qualified to give an opinion on a fellow cricketer. Of Briggs' bowling, the good doctor had to this to say in an interview: 'Briggs got most of his wickets with his leg breaks, especially when the ground was soft; but on good fast wickets I found the ball that gave me most trouble was the one he pitched on or just outside off stump and came in with his arm. This ball always made haste when it touched the ground and may have been a trifle faster than his ordinary slow medium.' In the same interview, Grace remembered the time when Briggs made the ball 'talk': 'In 1889 on the County Ground, Bristol, for Lancashire v Gloucestershire, he bowled as follows: Overs 16, maidens 9, runs 22, wickets 7. Five of these were clean bowled. I remember he was quite unplayable and I preferred to keep at the end Mold bowled at, and was not out 37 out of 87.' Grace's recollection of the game is spot-on save for the fact that the official Lancashire scorebook records that Briggs, in fact, bowled 16.4 overs.

And what about Briggs' temperament? Grace says: 'He was generally one of the best-tempered little fellows in the world. I remember on one occasion he was put out because his captain would not put him on, but eventually, when his turn came, he bowled his best.' Of his batting, Grace was slightly less complimentary, saying: 'Sometimes a very dangerous bat, but slashes and cuts immediately he gets to the wicket. Too often, caught in the slips.' Grace was later to remark that Briggs had 'the quickness of a cat' when it came to fielding his own bowling.

Another contemporary of Briggs, George Giffen, of Australia, was also full of praise for him after his debut Test against Giffen's countrymen at Lord's in 1886 – actually, it would have been hard not to be impressed by Briggs' debut which brought him 5 for 29 in the first innings and 6 for 45 in the second. Giffen, considered by many experts to have been one of the game's finest all-rounders, said: 'Merry Johnny' was then and for many years afterwards one of the most formidable of Australia's opponents, and had he been a more reliable batsman he would, to my mind, have ranked with A.G.Steel as an all-round player next to W.G. At his best he was a very fine bowler, one who was always worrying the batsman and always had to be watched.' Giffen had a point. Once established as a front-line bowler, Briggs was too often cavalier with the bat, trying to dominate the bowling from the very first ball he received without trying to build an innings. Of course, he came off plenty of times, but more often than not, he gave up his wicket for too few runs.

Lord Hawke, with whom Briggs had that celebrated spat during Briggs' benefit match, fondly recalled Briggs many years after that incident, saying: 'With a wicket to help him he could be a terror. He was a cheery, podgy soul, full of humour who perhaps played a little to the gallery, but never gave anything away.'

Digby Jephson, the Surrey captain between 1900 and 1902 and one of the last in a long line of lob bowlers, described Briggs bowling graphically: 'The ball left his hand with a finger flick that you could hear in the pavilion, and here was every known variety of flight... the ball was at you, spinning like a top; first a balloon of a ball that would drop much farther off than you thought, a lower one on just the same spot, both breaking away like smoke; then another, with nothing on, straight at the sticks.'

His county captain A.N. 'Monkey' Hornby had a high opinion of his teammate. Contributing a piece about Lancashire in 'The Jubilee Book of Cricket' by K.S.Ranjitsinhji, published in August 1897, Hornby wrote of Briggs: 'No better all-round man than Briggs, to sustain his form for so long, has ever represented us, and no one is known better all over the world. Very resourceful, he continues to maintain his position cleverly and there is plenty of cricket in him yet.'

Another cricketing great, C.B.Fry, wrote of Briggs: 'Why, he beams on you before and after your innings. The shorter your innings, the happier he is towards you. He passes you a cheery time of day. He inquires with feeling after your health and form. He rubs the ball in the dust, takes two steps and serves you a fast yorker instead of the high-tossed slow you expected. You retire. He smiles. What could be pleasanter?'

Lancashire's dressing room attendant W.E.Howard, who dealt with Briggs on a day to day basis, wrote of him: 'Both on and off the field, Johnny was full of high spirits and energy; it seemed impossible for him to remain stationary for a few seconds at a time. He was a great favourite; his quaint antics on the field were a source of amusement to the spectators and I should say he attracted more people to Old Trafford than any player I could mention. Possessed of enormous agility and stamina, he would frequently, after a hard day in the field, stop on his way home and play cricket with the youngsters in the fields. Johnny was not only a fine player; he had the reputation of being a bowler who assisted the umpires by not appealing for impossibilities. He was the finest fielder at cover-point I have seen; his anticipation of a batsman's stroke was great, while his agility enabled him to keep up his form almost to the end of his career.'

But perhaps Briggs was best summed up just 48 hours after his untimely death by his local newspaper, the *Manchester Guardian*, which wrote: 'Briggs for twenty years has been the very life of the cricket field. He has given cause of merriment, of surprise, of admiration to countless thousands of people. No bowler has had more cunning than he; none has shone more brightly in the place at cover slip; and before he became a great bowler he was famous as a batsman and till the very end of his career was never indifferent in that department of the game. He was an all-round player in the sense that Lohmann and Peel have been and that A.G.Steel was. He had his faults in a way that A.N.Hornby had his. In a way he played to the 'gallery'. He made a pretty presence with the bat, in the field and in bowling.'

And what did Briggs think about Briggs? In an interview in 1891, he said: 'I suppose I was really played for my batting in the first instance but I have always thought myself a better bowler than bat. Then, when a cricketer has been bowling any length of time and taking a responsible position in the field as cover point, he cannot be expected to make much off the bat.' 'I always feels satisfied if I come out first or second in the bowling analysis and have an average of 20-odd runs at the end of the season; that ought to be a satisfactory result for anybody.'

Briggs must have been pretty satisfied with his achievements – he averaged more than 20 with the bat eleven times and topped the Lancashire bowling averages on seven occasions. Eleven times he took more than 100 wickets in a season – a club record. Next in line is Dick Tyldesley with ten instances. Briggs was Lancashire's leading wicket-taker with 1,696 until overtaken by Brian Statham who reached 1,816 by the time of his retirement in 1968. There is no doubt that Briggs had a shrewd cricketing brain and as he once put it: 'It's not what ah do, it's what t'others think ah do as matters.'

So, starting as a fieldsman, becoming a batsman who could bowl and then a bowler who could bat, Briggs is difficult to categorise. However, unlike most sports, cricket throws up a veritable mountain of statistics and it is through these indisputable and irrefutable figures that one is able to put Briggs' career into a certain amount of perspective. Of course, there is the oft-repeated saw that 'there are lies, damned lies and statistics' but Briggs' runs and wickets add up to a formidable case on his behalf, although Cardus cautioned: 'We remember not the scorer and the results in after years; it is the men who remain in our minds, in our imagination.'

But it would be churlish to ignore Briggs' statistics, which in themselves tell a story of supreme dedication to his art. As a batsman, he amassed 14,902 first-class runs at an average of 18.27, scoring ten centuries, and his bowling brought him 2,221 wickets for 15.95 apiece. He claimed five wickets in an innings a remarkable two hundred times and achieved ten wickets in a match 41 times. In twelve of his seasons at Old Trafford he exceeded 100 wickets, five times going past 150. He is the only player to date to have scored more than 10,000 runs and taken 1,000 wickets for Lancashire. Only Brian Staham, with 761, has taken more than Briggs' 760 first-class wickets at Old Trafford. In the Test arena alone, he played 33 times for England, undertaking seven overseas tours – six of them to Australia – and scored 815 runs (average 18.11) with 118 wickets (average 17.74).

His stamina and his stoicism, particularly in the face of the illness which finally claimed him at such a young age, is not in doubt. There was always something happening or about to happen when Briggs was on a cricket field. He was an adornment to the game he loved – and the game and its supporters loved him. Briggs remained true to the spirit of the game until his dying day – and no one can say any more than that.

Appendix One
After Briggs' death

Briggs is buried in Stretford Cemetery, which lies at the end of a typically suburban road – Lime Road – almost exactly two miles from his cricketing home at Old Trafford. The cemetery, which was opened in 1885, is still in use today although there are few spaces still available. Briggs' grave lies about 150 yards from the chapel which is at the far end of the well-maintained cemetery. The stone is surmounted by a grey stone obelisk which towers over the other graves in its section. Interestingly, the inscription bears the name 'Johnny Briggs (Jack)'. Briggs is referred to as Jack is in the *Hornsea Gazette* report of his practice session with W.G.Grace many years earlier. He is also referred to as Jack in some contemporary Test match reports and in reports of his rugby exploits at Widnes. It is more than likely that Jack was the name which his wife and family must have called him.

Briggs is buried together with his wife Alice, who died in 1914, a daughter, Alice Nora, who survived her mother by only two months, and one of the twins, John Hector, who died in 1951 at the age of 67. At the base of the obelisk are sculptured two crossed bats, three stumps complete with bails, two balls and a Lancashire rose. Stretford Metrolink Station is close to the cemetery and trams – part of Manchester's light railway system – rattle on past the cemetery at regular intervals. Briggs might have been comforted to know that the next stop on the Altrincham-Bury route is Old Trafford Station, where passengers alight for the famous old cricket ground.

A fund was set up on behalf of Briggs' wife and family after his Leeds seizure, which according to a newspaper of the day, would allow 'his wife and Mrs Pilling (wife of wicket-keeper Dick Pilling) to carry on the business of Pilling and Briggs, a firm which deals with all athletic wares in Oxford Street, Manchester'. The sum of £740 was raised according to Lancashire's records.

Briggs' home at 15 Stamford Street, from where the hearse containing his body left on the day of his funeral, is still standing. It is in a fairly nondescript row of terraced houses at the end of which is an off-licence. The original outer brickwork and front door does not remain, however, as all the houses in the street appear to have been refurbished. There are two satellite dishes at the front of the house and no acknowledgement whatsoever that a famous cricketer ever lived there. The house is just over a mile from Old Trafford and it would have been a brisk twenty minute walk for Briggs to reach the ground on match days. The Briggs family were neighbours of Emma Pilling, widow of Lancashire wicket-keeper Dick Pilling, who resided two doors away at No.19. Briggs and her husband had been business partners, running a sports outfitters. Dick Pilling pre-deceased Briggs, dying from a lung condition on 28 March, 1891.

There was a Jack Briggs – no relation –who played for Lancashire in 1939, making four appearances. In four innings he failed to trouble the scorers, but was never dismissed. He took 10 wickets at an average of 39.10 with a best bowling of 4 for 48 against Derbyshire at Manchester.

Briggs appears on a set of 16 stamps issued in 1984 by the Pacific island of Tuvalu along with Arthur Shrewsbury, Hedley Verity and Patsy Hendren. Briggs, who features on two 60 cent stamps, is shown bowling and in portrait form. The island, which issues stamps known by some philatelists as 'wallpaper' and which are almost worthless, produced another cricketing set in the same year, featuring Brian Close, Geoffrey Boycott, David Bairstow and Godfrey Evans.

Little Johnny Briggs is mentioned along with 'Monkey' Hornby and others well-known cricketers of that era by a character in the 1985 book 'Sherlock Holmes at the 1902 Fifth Test' by Stanley Shaw. Written after the style of Sir Arthur Conan Doyle, the dramatis personae include Lord Hawke, Archie MacLaren, George Hirst and Wilfred Rhodes. Shaw, who also wrote 'Sherlock Holmes meets Annie Oakley', tells the rather preposterous tale of a young Australian visitor to London who is forced to bat at eleven for England in place of Rhodes in the final Test at The Oval, so that Holmes can solve the mystery of Rhodes' disappearance on the evening prior to the final day's play. The Australian ends up scoring the winning single in a last-wicket stand of 15 as England complete an astonishing victory. Throughout the book Holmes shows his distaste for cricket, calling it 'a waste of time' and describing it as an irrelevance. However, Conan Doyle himself was a cricket lover and a pretty good player to boot, appearing a number of times for MCC and playing in ten first-class fixtures in all between 1900 and 1907.

Appendix Two
Cricketers from Sutton-in-Ashfield

Players from Briggs' birthplace, Sutton-in-Ashfield, dominated the Victorian era of cricket in Nottinghamshire. There were so many from the village representing the county that it was dubbed "the nursery of cricket" and it even had its own society for professional cricketers. Apart from Briggs, who won more Test caps (33) than any other Sutton-born cricketer there were several others who represented Nottinghamshire and England including Fred Morley, William 'Billy' Barnes, Wilfred Flowers and George Bean.

Fred Morley played four times for England and it was during the 1882/83 tour of Australia that he injured his ribs but battled on to play his four representative matches. Soon afterwards his health deteriorated and he died the day after his benefit match started. The players carried on wearing black armbands. Morley is buried in Sutton-in-Ashfield cemetery.

William 'Billy' Barnes played 21 Tests, taking 51 wickets, making one century and two half centuries. He was a *Wisden* Cricketer of the Year in 1890, but his career was hampered by his fondness for a drink and he was frequently warned over his conduct. When his playing days were over he had a spell coaching at Lord's and then took over as the landlord of the Angel Inn in Mansfield Woodhouse.

Wilfred Flowers, although not born in Sutton, moved there from Calverton at an early age. He was the first professional player to score 1,000 first-class runs and take 100 wickets in a season and he played in eight Tests. He had a brief spell as a first-class umpire but was forced into early retirement when his eyesight began to fail.

George Bean played three times for England. He started off his cricketing career with Nottinghamshire but played only five times for them before moving on to Sussex where he spent 13 seasons. Nottinghamshire were to regret letting him go, particularly when he scored 145 and 92 not out against his former county. He might well have incurred the wrath of his ex-colleagues, but Sussex marked the occasion by giving him an inscribed silver cup. Like Morley, he was buried in Sutton-in-Ashfield cemetery, while other cricketing sons of the village also found their final resting place there. These included **Thomas 'Topsy' Wass**, whose bowling helped Nottinghamshire to the county championship in 1907. His career total was 1,666 wickets in 312 first-class games but although he played in a trial match, for an England XI and three times in Gentlemen v Players matches, he never made it into the full England Test team.

Also buried in Sutton cemetery is **Frank Farrands**, who played a handful of matches for Nottinghamshire as well as for Oxford, Ashbourne and Blackburn. After his playing career was over, Farrands became a respected first-class umpire.

James Shaw began his career in the pre-Test era, making his debut for Notts in 1865 and was regarded by W.G.Grace as the best fast bowler of the period. He was pretty fit, too, playing in every Nottinghmashire match in a ten-year period. He played for an England XI and it was against that England representative side that he produced the best bowling figures for a Nottinghamshire cricketer, 10 for 20.

Tom Buckland, whose birth was registered as Tom George Beastall, played twice for Nottinghasmshire with a highest score of 12 and best bowling of 2 for 13, while **John Kesteven** appeared in three games for Nottinghamshire and also a had a highest score of 12 while **William Marriott** also played twice for the county with a top score of 14 and 2 for 10 as his best bowling analysis. **Walter Price** had a more substantive career with 33 first-class appearances for MCC and Nottinghamshire, scoring 625 runs (highest score 57) and taking 15 wickets with a best return of 5 for 66 for MCC against Gloucestershire at Lord's in August 1870.

Also born in the village was **John Crossland**, who was to play in the same Lancashire team as Briggs. In all, Crossland played in 84 games for Lancashire between 1878 and 1887, but his career will mainly be remembered for controversy. His action was called into question on several occasions although he was never no-balled and he was also the centre of a row between Nottinghamshire and Lancashire over his eligibility to play for the Old Trafford side. In the end this finished his career as it was found that he did not have permanent residency in Lancashire and was thus ineligible to play for the county. Ironically, he was a resident of Lancashire, in

Blackburn, at the time of his death. His funeral was paid for by the Lancashire club.

There are two other Sutton-Lancashire links in the shape of **George Wharmby** and **Charles Shore**. Wharmby played for Lancashire in 1894 after playing four times for Nottinghamshire, while Shore, who started his career with Nottinghamshire, made one appearance for Lancashire and two for Liverpool and District before moving on to play in the Minor Counties with Norfolk.

Much more recently there was **Tim Robinson**, who captained the Trent Bridge side and played for England in 29 Tests and 26 one-day internationals. He made his Test debut against India at Mumbai in November 1984 and in the second Test of that tour scored a match-winning 160 at Delhi. He made two more big hundreds against Australia in the next series and looked on the cusp of greatness but didn't really recover from the working over he was given by West Indian pacemen Joel Garner and Malcolm Marshall and was never the same player again. He wasn't selected for the national side after he chose to tour South Africa with Mike Gatting's rebel side in 1989.

Latest off the Sutton 'production line' is Leicestershire's wicketkeeper-batsman **Tom New** who at the close of the 2006 season had made 18 first-class appearances for the Grace Road side, deputising for regular wicket-keeper Paul Nixon. New started his cricket with Mansfield Hosiery Mills CC in nearby Huthwaite and later captained the England youth team in the Costcutter Cup. His father, Martin, played in goal in 21 League games for Mansfield Town between 1978 and 1980. He also played in four other games, including three Anglo-Scottish Cup ties in one of which – coming on as a substitute against Partick Thistle – he was the Stags' hero, saving two penalties in a penalty shoot-out which Mansfield won 3-1. Swindon-born New, who started his football career as an apprentice with Arsenal, later played for Barnsley, Nuneaton Borough and Burton Albion. He was also an England schoolboy international.

Appendix Three
Career Statistics

Test Cricket: Batting and Fielding

		M	I	NO	R	HS	Ave	100	50	Ct
1884/85	(Australia)	5	7	0	177	121	25.28	1	-	3
1886	(Australia)	3	4	1	56	53	18.66	-	1	2
1886/87	(Australia)	2	4	0	71	33	17.75	-	-	1
1887/88	(Australia)	1	2	0	14	14	7.00	-	-	1
1888	(Australia)	3	4	1	39	22*	13.00	-	-	-
1888/89	(SA)	2	2	0	6	6	3.00	-	-	1
1891/82	(Australia)	3	5	0	124	41	24.80	-	-	1
1893	(Australia)	2	2	0	2	2	1.00	-	-	-
1894/95	(Australia)	5	9	0	164	57	18.22	-	1	3
1896	(Australia)	1	2	0	16	16	8.00	-	-	-
1897/98	(Australia)	5	9	3	146	46*	24.33	-	-	-
1899	(Australia)	1	-	-	-	-	-	-	-	-
Career		**33**	**50**	**5**	**815**	**121**	**18.11**	**1**	**2**	**12**

Test Cricket: Bowling

		Balls	M	R	W	BB	Ave	5i
1884/85	(Australia)	32	3	13	-	-	-	-
1886	(Australia)	537	75	132	17	6-45	7.76	2
1886/87	(Australia)	252	25	97	5	3-31	19.40	-
1888	(Australia)	337	42	94	12	5-25	7.83	1
1888/89	(South Africa)	391	51	101	21	8-11	4.80	2
1891/92	(Australia)	699	31	268	17	6-49	15.76	2
1893	(Australia)	601	40	293	16	5-34	18.31	2
1894/95	(Australia)	903	25	436	15	4-65	29.06	-
1896	(Australia)	290	26	123	3	2-99	41.00	-
1897/98	(Australia)	1140	57	485	9	3-96	53.88	-
1899	(Australia)	150	11	53	3	3-53	17.66	-
Career		**5332**	**386**	**2095**	**118**	**8-11**	**17.75**	**9**

Note: Overs were of four balls in Briggs' Test career in England in 1886 and 1888 and of five balls thereafter. Overseas, overs were of four balls until the end of his tour in South Africa in 1888/89 and six balls thereafter.

First-class Cricket: Batting and Fielding

		M	I	NO	R	HS	Ave	100	50	Ct
1879	(England)	5	8	0	73	36	9.12	-	-	1
1880	(England)	9	17	1	146	31*	9.12	-	-	5
1881	(England)	15	21	1	367	52	18.35	-	1	8
1882	(England)	20	32	4	287	30	10.25	-	-	7
1883	(England)	19	31	0	589	60	19.00	-	4	10
1884	(England)	22	36	2	667	112	19.61	1	2	15
1884/85	(Australia)	8	12	1	216	121	19.63	1	-	5
1885	(England)	20	33	2	857	186	27.64	2	5	15
1886	(England)	27	41	4	722	107	19.51	1	5	17
1886/87	(Australia)	11	17	0	319	86	18.76	-	3	6
1887	(England)	20	31	2	819	68	28.24	-	7	10
1887/88	(Australia)	8	13	1	229	75	19.08	-	2	7
1888	(England)	26	44	3	872	126*	21.26	1	4	11
1888/89	(SA)	2	2	0	6	6	3.00	-	-	1
1889	(England)	23	29	1	586	56	20.92	-	2	13
1890	(England)	26	42	4	708	129*	18.63	1	3	8
1891	(England)	21	31	1	371	68	12.36	-	1	9
1891/92	(Australia)	8	13	0	262	91	20.15	-	1	8
1892	(England)	22	34	0	569	115	16.73	1	2	6
1893	(England)	28	48	1	921	112	19.59	1	4	21
1894	(England)	23	35	0	675	101	19.28	1	4	8
1894/95	(Australia)	12	20	1	360	57	18.94	-	1	5
1895	(England)	23	34	2	367	49	11.46	-	0	9
1896	(England)	30	47	4	671	74	15.60	-	3	9
1897	(England)	28	38	2	636	74	17.66	-	1	21
1897/98	(Australia)	8	12	3	165	46*	18.33	-	-	1
1898	(England)	29	41	7	531	57*	15.61	-	1	10
1899	(England)	14	20	3	284	46	16.70	-	-	4
1900	(England)	28	44	5	817	58*	20.94	-	2	8
Career		**535**	**826**	**55**	**14092**	**186**	**18.27**	**10**	**58**	**258**

First-class Cricket: Bowling

		Balls	M	R	W	BB	Ave	5i	10m
1879	(Eng)	40	1	21	0	-	-	-	-
1880	(Eng)	371	48	96	9	5-34	10.66	1	-
1881	(Eng)	16	2	7	2	2-0	3.50	-	-
1882	(Eng)	310	32	127	6	4-11	21.16	-	-
1883	(Eng)	234	23	94	1	1-34	94.00	-	-
1884	(Eng)	1064	129	429	17	6-54	25.23	1	-
1884/85	(Aus)	32	3	13	0	-	-	-	-
1885	(Eng)	2596	325	921	67	9-29	13.74	8	2
1886	(Eng)	4734	622	1469	92	7-50	15.96	6	1
1886/87	(Aus)	2552	316	808	34	5-42	23.76	2	-
1887	(Eng)	6369	831	2018	114	7-44	17.70	9	1
1887/88	(Aus)	1485	205	434	30	6-40	14.46	2	1
1888	(Eng)	5802	763	1679	160	9-88	10.49	16	4
1888/89	(SA)	391	51	101	21	8-11	4.80	2	1
1889	(Eng)	5208	447	1647	140	7-22	11.76	14	3
1890	(Eng)	5568	456	1950	158	9-31	12.34	17	6
1891	(Eng)	4869	375	1693	128	8-46	13.22	14	4
1891/92	(Aus)	1212	71	420	32	6-49	13.12	4	1
1892	(Eng)	5225	438	1706	124	8-113	13.75	12	4
1893	(Eng)	6820	478	2639	166	8-19	15.89	17	6
1894	(Eng)	5421	376	2006	145	7-44	13.83	13	4
1894/95	(Aus)	2257	71	1058	44	5-97	24.04	1	-
1895	(Eng)	5547	413	2073	129	8-17	16.06	11	3

1896	(Eng)	8701	597	3253	165	7-59	19.71	17	3
1897	(Eng)	6465	401	2560	155	8-39	16.51	14	5
1897/98	(Aus)	1692	80	779	12	3-96	64.91	-	-
1898	(Eng)	4853	344	2025	83	8-63	24.39	5	-
1899	(Eng)	3336	247	1150	60	7-76	19.16	5	1
1900	(Eng)	6974	433	2254	127	10-55	17.74	9	2
Career		**100144**	**8578**	**35430**	**2221**	**10-55**	**15.95**	**200**	**52**

Note: In England, overs were of four balls from the start of Briggs' career in 1879 until the end of the 1888 season, five balls from 1889 to the end of the 1899 season, and six in 1900. Outside England , overs were of four balls until the end of his tour in South Africa in 1888/89 and six balls thereafter.

First-Class Cricket: Centuries (10)

1884	112	Lancashire	v Derbyshire, Old Trafford
1885/86	121	England	v Australia, Melbourne
1885	115	Lancashire	v Kent, Old Trafford
	186	Lancashire	v Surrey, Liverpool
1886	107	Lancashire	v Kent, Old Trafford
1888	126*	Lancashire	v Sussex, Old Trafford
1890	129*	Lancashire	v Sussex, Old Trafford
1892	115	Lancashire	v Yorkshire, Old Trafford
1893	112	Lancashire	v Surrey, The Oval
1894	101	Lancashire	v Kent, Tonbridge

First-Class Cricket: Six wickets in an innings (106)

	O	*M*	*R*	*W*	
1884	24	10	54	6	Lancashire v Somerset, Taunton
1885	17.2	2	49	6	Lancashire v Oxford University, Old Trafford
	46.2	25	71	6	Lancashire v Sussex, Hove
	21	14	23	6	Lancashire v MCC, Lord's
	41	15	76	6	Lancashire v MCC, Lord's
	42	29	29	9	Lancashire v Derbyshire, Derby
1886	38.1	17	45	6	England v Australia, Lord's
	38.1	15	50	7	Lancashire v Gloucestershire, Old Trafford
1887	26.3	13	36	6	Lancashire v Sussex, Old Trafford
	22.1	8	31	6	Lancashire v Oxford University, Liverpool
	51.1	32	44	7	Lancashire v Kent, Gravesend
	40	23	49	7	Lancashire v Derbyshire, Long Eaton
	58	31	53	7	Lancashire v Nottinghamshire, Old Trafford
1887/88	42.3	26	40	6	Shrewsbury's XI v Australian XI, Sydney
1888	60.3	27	88	9	Lancashire v Sussex, Old Trafford
	34.2	22	39	7	Lancashire v Middlesex, Old Trafford
	27.1	11	34	6	Lancashire v Middlesex, Old Trafford
	33	17	24	6	Lancashire v Yorkshire, Old Trafford
	15	9	13	6	Lancashire v Gloucestershire, Liverpool
	23	9	32	6	Lancashire v Gloucestershire, Liverpool
	42.1	27	33	6	Lancashire v Nottinghamshire, Old Trafford
	25.1	18	18	6	Londesborough's XI v Australians, Scarborough
	19.3	10	22	7	Londesborough's XI v Australians, Scarborough
	12	4	17	6	Shrewsbury's XI v Australians, Old Trafford
1888/89	19.1	11	17	7	England v South Africa, Cape Town
	14.2	5	11	8	England v South Africa, Cape Town
1889	28.3	10	56	6	Lancashire v Sussex, Old Trafford
	38.2	15	74	7	Lancashire v Middlesex, Old Trafford
	16.4	9	22	7	Lancashire v Gloucestershire, Bristol
	16	4	40	6	Lancashire v Gloucestershire, Liverpool
	27.4	9	56	6	Lancashire v Surrey, The Oval

	14	6	18	6	Pilling's XI v Hall's XI, Holbeck
1890	18.3	5	33	7	Laverton's XI v Australians, Westbury
	28.1	8	60	6	Lancashire v Surrey, Old Trafford
	12	4	26	6	Lancashire v Middlesex, Lord's
	70	32	107	6	Lancashire v Nottinghamshire, Trent Bridge
	44.2	25	44	8	Lancashire v Nottinghamshire, Old Trafford
	35.1	15	44	7	North of England v Australians, Leeds
	29.1	16	31	9	Londesborough's XI v Australians, Scarborough
	24.2	14	26	6	Londesborough's XI v Australians, Scarborough
1891	51	16	80	6	Lancashire v Yorkshire, Bradford
	51	16	104	6	Players v Gentlemen, The Oval
	41	17	76	6	Lancashire v Yorkshire, Old Trafford
	35.1	18	46	8	Lancashire v Yorkshire, Old Trafford
	34	12	56	7	Lancashire v Surrey, The Oval
	31	15	63	7	North v South, Scarborough
1891/92	21.5	4	49	6	England v Australia, Adelaide
	28	7	87	6	England v Australia, Adelaide
1892	29	15	32	7	Lancashire v Oxford University, Oxford
	36.1	15	60	6	Lancashire v Nottinghamshire, Trent Bridge
	23	9	26	7	Lancashire v Somerset, Taunton
	48.4	10	113	8	Lancashire v Yorkshire, Old Trafford
	24	6	62	7	Lancashire v Somerset, Old Trafford
	30.3	12	73	6	Lancashire v Surrey, The Oval
1893	30.2	12	46	7	Lancashire v Oxford University, Oxford
	59.2	25	87	8	Lancashire v Kent, Old Trafford
	56	20	114	6	Lancashire v Australians, Old Trafford
	22.4	8	35	6	Lancashire v Nottinghamshire, Trent Bridge
	15	8	19	8	Lancashire v Yorkshire, Leeds
	16	3	45	6	Lancashire v Somerset, Liverpool
	41.1	17	64	6	Lancashire v Surrey, The Oval
	28.2	8	47	8	Lancashire v Gloucestershire, Old Trafford
	22	8	35	6	Lancashire v Yorkshire, Old Trafford
1894	54	25	55	6	Lancashire v Kent, Old Traford
	21	6	44	7	Lancashire v Oxford University, Oxford
	30	10	52	6	Lancashire v Oxford University, Old Trafford
	37.3	14	71	7	Lancashire v Somerset, Taunton
	22	12	27	6	Lancashire v Leicestershire, Old Trafford
	31	8	91	7	Lancashire v Yorkshire, Bradford
	34	16	46	7	Lancashire v Surrey, The Oval
	28.4	11	47	6	Lancashire v Surrey, The Oval
1895	43	18	74	6	Lancashire v Sussex, Old Trafford
	24	5	49	8	Lancashire v Gloucestershire, Old Trafford
	35	15	43	6	Lancashire v Surrey, The Oval
	42.1	19	67	7	Lancashire v Nottinghamshire, Old Trafford
	24.1	17	17	8	Lancashire v Leicestershire, Leicester
1896	60.1	20	93	7	Lancashire v Gloucestershire, Bristol
	27.1	7	41	6	North of England v Australians, Old Trafford
	40	25	38	6	Lancashire v Somerset, Old Trafford
	26.2	9	59	7	Lancashire v Gloucestershire, Old Trafford
	66	29	110	7	Lancashire v Leicestershire, Leicester
	90	32	185	6	Lancashire v Derbyshire, Old Trafford
	26.1	11	44	6	Lancashire v Surrey, The Oval
	38	12	63	7	Lancashire v Australians, Liverpool
1897	63.2	19	135	6	Lancashire v MCC, Lord's
	28.3	12	39	7	Lancashire v Leicestershire, Leicester
	39	16	70	8	Lancashire v Derbyshire, Liverpool
	22	8	35	6	Lancashire v Gloucestershire, Liverpool
	19	3	39	8	Lancashire v Hampshire, Old Trafford
	32	13	55	6	Lancashire v Kent, Canterbury
	42	14	80	7	Lancashire v Kent, Canterbury
	20	5	43	6	Lancashire v Leicestershire, Old Trafford
	43.4	17	67	6	Lancashire v Surrey, The Oval

	36	12	48	6	Lancashire v Middlesex, Lord's
1898	22	6	68	6	Lancashire v Hampshire, Old Trafford
	34	9	63	8	Lancashire v Middlesex, Old Traford
	31.2	7	82	7	Lancashire v Sussex, Old Trafford
1899	39	11	77	6	Lancashire v Hampshire, Southampton
	48.3	12	109	6	Lancashire v Somerset, Taunton
	39	12	76	7	Lancashire v Yorkshire, Sheffield
1900	28.5	7	55	10	Lancashire v Worcestershire, Old Trafford
	40.3	13	87	7	Lancashire v Middlesex, Lord's
	54.3	22	95	6	Lancashire v Warwickshire, Edgbaston
	39	24	53	7	Lancashire v Nottinghamshire, Old Trafford
	23	8	49	6	Lancashire v Leicestershire, Old Trafford
	33.5	8	135	6	North of England v South of England, Lord's

Notes: (a) In England, overs were of four balls from the start of Briggs' career in 1879 until the end of the 1888 season, five balls from 1889 to the end of the 1899 season, and six in 1900. Outside England, overs were of four balls until the end of his tour in South Africa in 1888/89 and six balls thereafter. (b) Briggs took in addition, five wickets in an innings 94 times in first-class matches, the best being 5 for 11 for Lancashire v Oxford University, Old Trafford, 1885.

Milestones

3 October, 1862: Born at Sutton-in-Ashfield, Nottinghamshire.

1875: Briggs family moved to Widnes, giving their son a residential qualification for Lancashire.

May, 1876: Joined Hornsea CC in East Yorkshire as a professional, aged 13.

May, 1878: Joined Northern CC in Liverpool as a professional, still aged only 15.

26-28 May, 1879: Played debut first-class match, for Lancashire against Nottinghamshire at Trent Bridge, aged 16 years 235 days, scoring 36 and taking 0 for 13 in a drawn match.

31 July, 1880: Took five wickets in an innings for first time in first-class cricket, with 5 for 34 in the second innings, playing as a 'given man' for Gentlemen of the North against Players of the North at Old Traffor 1.

27 August, 1881: Completed first full season for Lancashire, playing in fifteen first-class matches for the county.

22 May, 1884: Scored first century in first class cricket, 112 in Lancashire's first innings against Derbyshire at Old Trafford.

12 August, 1884: Took five wickets in an innings for the first time in a county match, 6 for 54 in Somerset's second innings at Taunton.

19 September, 1884: Joined A.Shaw's XI at Plymouth, at the start of his first overseas tour, to Australia.

12-16 December, 1884: Played debut Test match, against Australia at Adelaide, scoring 1 in his only innings, but did not bowl.

1 and 2 January, 1885: Scored century in his second Test, 121 in England's first innings at Melbourne, his highest score in Test cricket.

6 and 7 July, 1885: Played in his first match for Players against Gentlemen at Lord's, scoring 21 and 12, but did not bowl.

16 and 17 July, 1885: Scored 186 in Lancashire's first innings against Surrey at The Oval, his highest score in first class cricket, adding 173 for tenth wicket with Dick Pilling, setting a new world first-class record for the last wicket.

4 and 5 August, 1885: Took 9 for 29 in Derbyshire's second innings at Derby, his best innings return in first-class cricket until 1900.

5-7 July, 1886: Played in his first Test match in England, against Australia at Old Trafford, scoring 1 and 2*, but did not bowl.

19-21 July, 1886: Played in his first Test match at Lord's, against Australia, scoring 0, but took 5 for 29 and 6 for 45.

18 September 1886: Joined A.Shaw's XI at Plymouth, at the start of his second tour to Australia.

19 August, 1887: In taking 7 for 53 in Nottinghamshire's second innings, reached 100 first-class wickets in season for the first time.

7 September, 1887: Joined A.Shrewsbury's XI at Plymouth, at the start of his third tour to Australia, later travelling on to New Zealand.

21 November 1888: Joined R.G.Warton's XI in London, at the start of his first tour to South Africa.

25 and 26 March 1889: Took 15 wickets for 28 in Second Test against South Africa at Cape Town, the best fifteen wicket match return by any bowler in Test cricket.

April, 1889: Identified by *Wisden* as one of its first set of Cricketers of the Year.

30 June, 1 and 2 July, 1890: Playing for Lancashire against Sussex at Old Trafford, scored 129* and then took 5 for 25 and 5 for 16.

2 October 1891: Joined Lord Sheffield's XI in London, at the start of his fourth tour to Australia.

2 February 1892: Took Test match hat-trick in Australia's second innings at Sydney.

24-28 March, 1892: Took 12 for 129 in Test Match at Adelaide, his best match return against Australia: during the first innings of this match he reached his 1,000th first-class wicket.

1-3 August, 1892: Playing for Lancashire against Yorkshire at Old Trafford, scored 115 and then took 8 for 113 and 5 for 96.

11 August 1893: Twins born to his wife, while he was playing for Lancashire's Second XI at Stourbridge.

14 and 15 May, 1894: Awarded benefit match against Yorkshire at Old Trafford, but this was completed in two days.

30 June, 1894: Reached 10,000th first-class run, while scoring 22 for Lancashire in their second innings against Kent at Tonbridge.

21 September, 1894: Joined A.E.Stoddart's XI at Tilbury at the start of his fifth tour to Australia.

1 February, 1895: Playing in his 25th Test match, at Sydney, became first bowler to take 100 Test wickets, with 4 for 65 in Australia's only innings.

17 October, 1897: Joined A.E.Stoddart's XI at Tilbury at the start of his sixth tour to Australia.

7 July, 1898: Reached 2,000th first-class wicket, while taking 7 for 34 for Lancashire in the Sussex first innings at Old Trafford, only the second player to reach this total.

5-7 June 1899: Played 500th first-class match, for Lancashire against Warwickshire at Edgbaston.

29 June, 1899: Played in Test match for England v Australia at Leeds, taking 3 for 53, but suffered an epileptic seizure after the end of first day's play.

8 July, 1899: Admitted to Cheadle Royal Lunatic Asylum for first time.

28 March, 1900: Discharged from hospital, having made a good recovery.

7 and 8 May, 1900: Played first first-class match since leaving hospital, for Lancashire against Hampshire at Old Trafford, scoring 19, but did not bowl.

24 May, 1900: In his fourth first-class match since leaving hospital, after Worcestershire had elected to bat, took 10 for 55 in the visitors' first innings at Old Trafford, the best innings return of his career.

30 and 31 August and 1 September, 1900: Played last match for Lancashire, against Leicestershire at Old Trafford, scoring 36* and taking 2 for 42 and 6 for 49.

14 -16 September, 1900: Played final first-class match, at Lord's for North of England v South of England, taking five wickets in an innings for 200th time.

8 March, 1901: Re-admitted to Cheadle Royal Lunatic Asylum.

11 January, 1902: Died in hospital at Cheadle, aged 39 years 100 days.

Acknowledgements and Bibliography

Despite his colourful life and times, only three books on Briggs had been published up to 2006. The first was a contemporary account, entitled 'The Life of John Briggs', written by Herbert Turner with sketches by Rip and selling for 2p. It was originally published in 1902 by Thomas Sowler and Sons Ltd of Cannon Street, Manchester. A second, enlarged and revised edition, also selling for 2p, was also published. At the time *Cricket* magazine described it as 'very cheap at the price'. In 2000 it was reprinted in facsimile edition by Red Rose Books with a new introduction by Gerry Wolstenholme. Only 200 numbered copies were produced. The second book, 'Johnny Remembered, a celebration of the life and career of Johnny Briggs', was written by the Rev Malcolm Lorimer, a former chairman of the ACS. It was published in 2006 in a limited edition of 225 copies. Lorimer, although born in Yorkshire, has been involved with Lancashire for more than twenty years in many capacities, including as the club's honorary chaplain. In the latter capacity he once organised a prayer room for Moslems to be used during a one-day international at Old Trafford involving Pakistan. Lorimer is also the club's official historian and archivist.

The most recently published book on Briggs is 'Johnny Briggs: Ashes century, Ashes hat-trick' by K Martin Tebay. Again Red Rose Books was responsible for this limited edition of 200 copies, which first appeared in November 2006.

Shortly after Briggs died a pamphlet listing a complete record of his performances in county cricket was published in Manchester. It was available from the author, Mr T. Swindell, 'post free for twopence', from his home address in Morton Road, Eccles.

Of course, articles and photographs of Briggs appeared in contemporary cricket magazines and other publications, including *Wisden's Cricketers' Almanack* (1889), *English Illustrated Magazine* (June, 1890), *Cricket* magazine (26 February, 1885, 14 August, 1890, 25 September, 1890, 23 August, 1894, and 30 January,

1902), *English Sports* (2 September, 1893), *Cricket Field* newspaper (12 May, 1894) and *Bailey's Magazine* (June, 1895).

Briggs' nephew, Jim Briggs, of Leamington Spa, Warwickshire, was a collector of Briggs cricketana. Unfortunately, his collection was lost after his death in the 1970s.

In November 2005, BBC Radio 4's *Making History* programme featured an item about Briggs, presented by Sue Cook and featuring Malcolm Lorimer. Cook, talking about England's forthcoming tour to Pakistan told listeners that 'Andrew "Freddie" Flintoff came from a long line of successful Lancastrian cricketers, but none has a story as moving as Johnny Briggs'. Reporter Ivan Howlett, who visited Old Trafford and Briggs' grave at Stretford Cemetery during the course of the programme, described Briggs as 'a hero on the same scale as Lancashire's Andrew Flintoff'.

I have consulted the following books:

Don Ambrose, *Liverpool & District Cricketers 1882-1947*, 2002 (ACS Publication)

Jean Barclay, *A Caring Community*, 1992

R.G.Barlow, *Forty Seasons of First-Class Cricket*, 1908, re-printed 2002

C.J.Bartlett, *Eddie Paynter: His Record Innings-by-Innings*, 2006 (ACS Publication)

Brian Bearshaw, *From the Stretford End*, 1990

Derek Birley, *A Social History of English Cricket*, 1999

Robert Brooke and David Goodyear, *A Who's Who of Lancashire Cricket*, 1991

Neville Cardus, *Days in the Sun*, 1924

Roy Cavanagh, *The White Flash*, undated

Joseph Connolly, *The Treatment of the Insane without Mechanical Constraint*, 1856

Michael Down, *Archie*, 1981

David Frith, *England versus Australia*, 1993

David Frith, *The Slow Men*, 1984

W.G.Grace, *WG: Cricketing Reminiscences and Personal Recollections*, 1899 (re-printed 1980)

Dean Hayes, *Lancashire County Cricket Club: an A-Z*, 1997

Keith Hayhurst, *A pictorial history of Lancashire County Cricket Club*, 2000

W.E.Howard, *Fifty Years' Cricket Reminiscences of a Non-Player*, 1928

John Kay, *A History of County Cricket: Lancashire*, 1972

Malcolm Lorimer, *Johnny Remembered,* 2006

Malcolm Lorimer et al, *Lancashire County Cricket Club First-Class Records 1865-1998,* 1999

Malcolm Lorimer and Don Ambrose, *Lancashire Cricketers 1865-1988,* 1989 (ACS Publication)

Mike Marqusee, *Anyone but England* (Second Edition), 1998

Douglas Miller, *A History of Bucks County Cricket Club,* 2006 (ACS Publication)

Rex Pogson, *Lancashire,* 1952

K.S.Ranjitsinhji, *The Jubilee Book of Cricket,* 1897

Stanley Shaw, *Sherlock Holmes at the 1902 Fifth Test,* 1985

K.M.Tebay, *Johnny Briggs: Ashes Century, Ashes Hat-Trick,* 2006

Herbert Turner, *The Life of John Briggs,* 1902

Rob Wadsworth, *Ashfield: The Nursery of Cricket,* 2002

Peter Wynne-Thomas: *England on Tour: Record of all England Cricket Tours Overseas,* 1982.

I have consulted other publications, including *Wisden Cricketers' Almanack* (various); *The Cricketer* (various); *Cricket* magazine (various); *Weekly Times* (various); *Leeds Evening Express* (various); *Manchester Guardian* and *The Guardian* (various); *Manchester Evening News* (various); *Oldham Chronicle*; *City News* (various); *Athletic Journal*; *Athletic News Cricket Annual* (various); *Lillywhite's Cricket Annual* (various); *Hornsea Gazette*; *Lancashire CCC Yearbooks* (various), and *Playfair Cricket Annuals* (various). In addition, I used several websites, including answers.com; cricketarchive.com; cricinfo.com; cricmania.com; google.com; icc-cricket.com; lccc.co.uk; nottsccc.co.uk; widnesvikings.co.uk; wccc.co.uk; sulekha.com; wikipedia.org, and 123india.com.

My special thanks to Douglas Miller, chairman of the Association of Cricket Statisticians and Historians, who encouraged me to undertake this project and to the ACS's indefatigable David Jeater, editor of the *Lives in Cricket* series, who provided me with a wealth of information on Briggs and spotted numerous errors, which thankfully have been corrected; Roger Mann, who supplied many of the pictures in the book; Don Ambrose; Malcolm Lorimer, who gave me a great deal of help with newspaper and magazine cuttings and also supplied some of the photographs; Peter Wynne-Thomas; Margaret Thomas of the National Society for Epilepsy; Widnes Vikings historian Steve Fox; Mansfield Town historian Paul Taylor; philatelist Martin Lipczer; David Atkinson; Simon Brodbeck of the *Daily Express*, who read the proofs and made several helpful suggestions, and last but not least my long-suffering wife Bella, who had to put up with my long, often late hours at the computer. I would like therefore to dedicate this book to her and to our four cricket-loving children, Alex, Oscar, Edgar and Edward.